# REPORT OF THE DIRECTOR GENERAL OF TELECOMMUNICATIONS

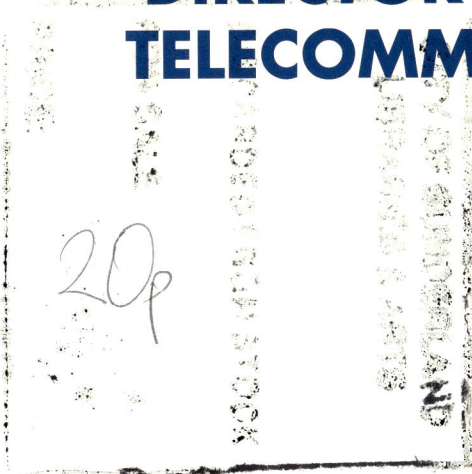

to the Secretary of State
for Trade and Industry
for the period 1 January
to 31 December 1998

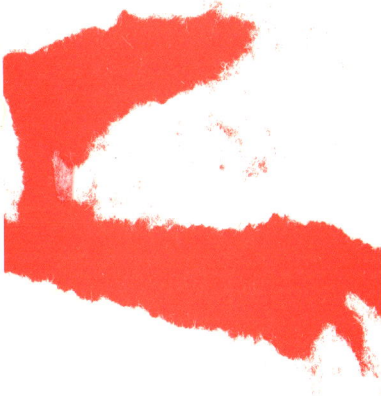

PRESENTED TO PARLIAMENT
IN PURSUANCE OF SECTION 55 OF
THE TELECOMMUNICATIONS ACT 1984

ORDERED BY THE HOUSE OF COMMONS
TO BE PRINTED 29 APRIL 1999

LONDON: THE STATIONERY OFFICE

£28

HC 393

**CONTENTS**

The Rt Hon Stephen Byers, MP
Secretary of State for Trade and Industry
1 Victoria Street
London     SW1H OET

19 April 1999

Dear Stephen,

As Director General of Telecommunications I am required by section 55 of the Telecommunications Act 1984, to make to you an annual report for each calendar year on my activities and the activities of the Monopolies and Mergers Commission (MMC) in so far as they relate to references made by me.

I enclose my report for the period 1 January to 31 December 1998.

In the first part of the report I comment on our progress in key areas during 1998 and our aims for future years. Part Two describes OFTEL's activities during the year which include protecting the interests of consumers and promoting effective competition. Part Three contains the reports of the seven statutory advisory committees on telecommunications.

In March 1998 I referred the issue of calls to mobile phones to the MMC to investigate whether the level of charges were against the public interest. They agreed with our view and OFTEL has since taken action to cut the price of these calls, which will save customers £1 billion over the next three years.

Yours sincerely,

D A EDMONDS
Director General

# Director General's Statement

1.1 This has been my first year as Director General of Telecommunications. It has been exciting and challenging. As ever, developments in the telecommunications industry seemed to happen at an ever-faster pace, with new services and new ways of paying for these services stimulating growth.

1.2 Huge growth has been experienced in the use of mobile phones, particularly for personal use, stimulated by the introduction of pre-pay deals. The introduction of subscription-free access to the Internet has led to greater use of the world wide web, both for accessing information and purchasing goods. There has been a massive increase in data traffic across networks, as businesses increasingly use telecommunications to carry text information. Most European Union Member States opened up their telecommunications markets to competition on 1 January 1998, in accordance with EU liberalisation measures. This has resulted in wider choice for consumers and wider commercial opportunities for telecommunications companies.

1.3 All this means that telecommunications has ever greater importance in our society, both commercially and socially. OFTEL has to play a key role in creating a competitive telecommunications market that meets customers needs. This is the prime objective of the efforts of the hardworking and dedicated staff at OFTEL. 1998 saw some real achievements and positive steps that are described in this report.

## Working for the customer

1.4 There was a huge effort in the past year by our team investigating the price of calls to mobile phones. Our initial investigations led us to believe that there was scope for the mobile phone companies Cellnet and Vodafone, and BT to make considerable price reductions. Following our reference, the Monopoly and Mergers Commission agreed with our conclusions. This allowed us to put in place a new price control, which will save £1 billion for customers over the next three years. The first results of this should be seen in consumers' bills from April 1999.

1.5 A further example of OFTEL's consumer work was the introduction, on January 1 1999, of mobile number portability. For the first time customers unhappy with their mobile provider can move to an alternative supplier and retain their original number. Customers can shop around for the best deal. The UK is the first country in the world to give customers this ability.

1.6 Junk faxes and unwanted telesales calls have been at the top of the complaints-to-OFTEL league for most of the year even though there are codes of practice and other voluntary rules in place to protect customers. The sending of unwanted faxes is a particular source of irritation to many people, and others are infuriated by the interruption caused by telesales calls to their homes or businesses. People should not be harassed by telesales calls after clearly telling the caller they do not want to be phoned again. Last year I banned one company from making such calls. The intention was to send a clear message to all companies involved in telesales that this behaviour will not be tolerated.

1.7 OFTEL will continue to enforce licence obligations whenever necessary. 1999 will see the introduction of a new obligatory scheme, which will be enforced by the Data Protection Registrar. Individuals can only be sent faxes with their prior consent and business can opt out from receiving junk faxes altogether. I am sure these new measures, which come into force on 1 May, will be welcomed by customers and all reputable direct marketing companies.

1.8 Last year saw the start of the publicity campaign funded by all the telephone companies to make businesses aware of the national code and number changes that will take place in 2000. Giving businesses plenty of time will help minimise their costs - for example when stationary has to be reordered, the new numbers can be included in their letterhead.

1.9 OFTEL is well aware that changing telephone numbers is never welcome, but the huge explosion in demand for faxes, mobile phones and modems for computers has meant some areas are in danger of running out of telephone numbers. OFTEL consulted on the options in 1995 and in the light of comments received, we chose the option that was most acceptable to consumers and met their requirement for clear and consistent numbering.

1.10 The changes will do two things. First, it will create a huge store of new numbers for the future. Second, it will provide a clear structure for phone services such as mobiles, pagers, and special rate services. People will know what service they are dialling and in what range the charge is likely to be.

1.11 An important part of OFTEL's work is to ensure the delivery of affordable basic telecommunications services to all consumers including those with disabilities. Last year OFTEL issued a consultation document and statement on the measures that telecommunications companies should put in place to ensure that people with disabilities have proper access to the sorts of telecommunications services which most people take for granted. These included publicising the services for people with disabilities in appropriate ways and providing a free directory information service for people who cannot use a phone directory. The statement also included measures designed to improve the ease of use of textphones for people with impaired hearing, and measures to improve access to public payphones. The DTI are still considering OFTEL's proposals and should be drafting a Statutory Instrument to bring them into effect in the near future.

1.12 Unfortunately, 1998 also saw the failure of the network operator Ionica, which provided a telephony service using fixed radio links. As soon as we were informed of problems, OFTEL worked closely with the administrators to ensure that Ionica customers were able to transfer to BT or a cable company where one was available. Our prime concern was to ensure the continuity of supply of telephone services, with particular emphasis on business customers who faced the loss of advertised telephone numbers. This was the first failure of a telecommunications company that OFTEL has had to deal with.

## Better information means better deals

1.13 There is a need for clear and accurate price information so that consumers can compare like with like. For far too long customers have been faced by a baffling array of prices, which means that their ability to compare performance is limited.

1.14 The publication of comparative data, either on a standardised basis agreed by the industry, or if necessary required by the regulator independently is a priority in the telecommunications sector. We gained agreement in 1998 by the industry to a methodology. It has taken longer than I had wished, but we are pushing ahead with this work, and results will be published in 1999.

1.15 It is important to stress that customers should not only rely on prices when selecting telecommunications providers. It is vital that issues such as quality of service are taken into account. 1998 has seen more and more fixed telecommunications companies taking part in the publication of Comparative Performance Indicators which address quality issues such as billing accuracy and the speedy repair of faults. A total of 17 took part in November and three more have pledged their support to the process.

1.16 We hope to build on this with the production of better and clearer data on the prices, quality and coverage offered by mobile networks. OFTEL has shown the way by the publication of our own 'snapshot survey' of the four networks and we will be pushing hard for similar work by the networks themselves and publication of independent data in 1999.

1.17 In November, OFTEL published our own proposals for publishing information about the complaints that we receive. The number of complaints and enquiries we receive has risen from 42,000 in 1997 to 50,000 in 1998. From summer 1999 we will be publishing data about the top 10 complaints we receive and name the companies that customers are complaining about. These proposals all support OFTEL's contention that an informed customer is an empowered customer.

1.18 OFTEL's website continues to grow as the principal channel of informing the industry, analysts, and increasingly the public, of our work. The number of 'hits' to OFTEL's home page was 201,485 in 1998, double the number of the previous year. New publications appearing on our website always generates interest, but the site also contains a comprehensive source of background material on our work.

## Working together for the customer's benefit

1.19 There have been three important developments over the year. First, in 1998 the new Competition Act received Royal Assent. OFTEL, and other regulators, have been given powers concurrent with the OFT. Joint preparatory work has been started to ensure consistency in application of the new powers when they come into effect in March 2000. OFTEL is seeking to draw back from detailed prescriptive regulation whenever possible. But there are many occasions where there is a need to act to protect consumers' interests to prevent anti-competitive behaviour. It is also important that the regulators are seen to be consistent in their application of the new powers brought in by the Act.

1.20 Second, boundaries between broadcasting, telecommunications and IT are becoming increasingly blurred. It is increasingly important that the OFT, OFTEL and the ITC work together to address regulatory issues concerning these sectors. So in 1998 the 'group of three' was established to enable a unified approach to common regulatory issues.

1.21 Third, the Millennium 'bug'. OFTEL is playing a major role with the telecommunications industry, which has spent two years addressing this issue with total openness. Operators have been united through the Telecommunications Operators Forum to identify potential problems, share experience and swap solutions. They have also been active in inspecting each other's preparations and agreeing contingency schemes, along with OFTEL. UK telecommunications companies have been at the forefront of international efforts to address Y2K compliance through the work of the International Telecommunication Union. UK telecommunications networks are on course for 'business as usual' through the date change.

## Ensuring the UK's voice is heard in Europe

1.22 There are major challenges ahead for everyone involved in telecommunications. Primary among them is the European Union review of telecommunications legislation.

1.23 OFTEL and the Department of Trade and Industry have begun a joint initiative to address the interests of all those involved in the industry – from ordinary phone users to the industry itself. We will be working together throughout 1999 to ensure that the interests of the UK are heard as the debate unfolds in Brussels. One major workshop has already been held and other events are planned. It is vital that everyone with an interest in the telecommunications sector of the UK contributes to this exercise – waiting until the legislation has been formed is too late.

1.24 There was a substantial amount of work by OFTEL over the year to bring the UK's licences for telecommunications services into line with the EU's Licensing Directive. The Directive is a key part of the process of liberalisation and creates a common framework for licensing that is transparent and non-discriminatory. All new licenses issued from 1 January 1998 had to comply with the directive, and in addition over 400 existing UK licences had to be amended by OFTEL, working closely with the companies concerned.

## Preparing for the challenges of the Information Age

1.25 One of the most important publications from OFTEL in 1998 was our consultation document on Access to Bandwidth. This document asked a number of key questions about the future of the "final mile" of the telecommunications network – that is the link from street boxes to home or small business. While recognising that competition is increasing and cable companies will soon be offering service to 50% of the population, BT is still the dominant operator in the local domestic network. This 'final mile' is becoming increasingly important as we look to the provision of information age services – such as faster Internet access – to the home and small business. The consultation discusses whether there are any blocks at present to the provision of higher bandwidth services to residential customers and smaller businesses. It asks that if blocks exist, what action is needed to overcome them. The responses to our consultation will play an important part in the debate that OFTEL has fostered. This issue will be a key area for our work in next year as we ensure that customers can gain access to Information Age services.

## Getting into shape for the challenges to come

1.26 Fundamental changes have been made to OFTEL's organisation as we prepare to meet the challenges of the future and take up our new role as a competition authority. The emphasis has been to prepare OFTEL for events in the coming years.

1.27 Soon after taking up my post as Director General I launched a review of OFTEL's structure. This was to find out whether our people and our financial resources were being used as efficiently as possible. It also sought to highlight best practice in the private sector and identify ways that their adoption could help OFTEL to make decisions of a consistently high quality. The review was carried out with the help of external consultants and with the active participation and leadership of OFTEL staff.

1.28 We decided that the old structure was too fragmented and "departmental" reflecting a traditional 'Civil Service' approach with 10 different branches. We have now created a new, more agile organisation with the old branches replaced by three directorates: Regulatory Policy and Compliance, backed up by Business Support.

1.29 This slimmed-down structure is better suited to meet the needs of everyone who relies upon the modern communications industry. It puts the interest of the consumer at the heart of everything we do and, as our work programme shows, helps us to operate in a more integrated way. Change happens on an almost daily basis in the fast-moving world of telecommunications and it is vital that OFTEL is equipped to meet these new challenges as they arise.

1.30  1998 has been a dynamic year. We have sought to work with the industry in a business-like way, without compromising our responsibility to the consumer. Now we also have a more flexible structure that ensures that we use our experience to deliver solutions that help the consumer and are right for the industry well into the new millennium.

*OFTEL's Executive Board: Jane Whittles (Director of Compliance), Anne Lambert (Director of Operations), David Smith (Director of Business Support), David Edmonds (Director General) and Ann Taylor (Director of Regulatory Policy).*

# OFTEL'S Chronology of Events – 1998

---

## JANUARY

---

- OFTEL published Beyond the Telephone, the Television and the PC – II, its first submission to the Culture Media and Sports Select Committee Inquiry into audio-visual communications and the regulation of broadcasting.

- OFTEL announced that Coventry's code will change from 01203 to 024 in 2000 in order to meet projected demand for new numbers in the city. The new code will give a ten-fold increase in the supply of numbers in the Coventry area.

---

## FEBRUARY

---

- OFTEL set out guidelines in Effective Competition Review on how it will respond to competition issues in the UK telecommunications market.

- The statement Identification of Significant Market Power for the Purposes of the Interconnection Directive was issued. This explained the methodology OFTEL used in determining that four operators (BT, Kingston, Cellnet and Vodafone) have Significant Market Power.

- OFTEL issued a statement Improving Accountability: Further Steps. This explained a series of new measures designed to ensure that OFTEL's work is even more accountable and transparent in the future.

- New rules were issued on charges to broadcasters for access to digital set-top boxes. Details are set out in the document Conditional Access Charges for Digital Television.

- Cellnet was told to stop unfair pricing towards some of its service providers. A provisional order was made against the mobile phone company.

- A consultation on payphone provision was launched. The document A Better Deal for Payphone Users set out the types of services the public should be able to obtain in a payphone.

- OFTEL launched a new initiative to promote telecoms for all. The consultative document Telecommunications Services for People with Disabilities set out clear duties on operators to provide facilities and services for disabled customers that are available for any other user.

## MARCH

◆ A major review was launched to ensure that Hull gains the full benefits of the information age. The consultative document Delivering the Benefits of the Information Age top Customers in Hull contained the full details. Following publication OFTEL held a public meeting in Hull on 25 March to hear the views of local people and businesses.

◆ OFTEL's Director General, Don Cruickshank announced that he had asked the Monopolies and Mergers Commission (MMC) to investigate the price of calling mobile phones. Details were contained in the document Prices of Calls to Mobile Phones.

◆ Don Cruickshank, gave a speech to The Economist entitled 'Enhancing Profitability within Telecoms' on the reform of regulation of the electronic communications industry.

◆ Don Cruickshank gave OFTEL's second submission to the Culture, Media and Sport Select Committee, Beyond the Telephone, the Television and the PC – Regulation of the Electronic Communications Industry. He called for the industry to be regulated by two new bodies, an Electronics Communications Commission, responsible for competition, economic and social policy issues, including consumer protection, and an Electronic Communications Standards Authority, responsible for content regulation, including public service broadcasting.

◆ The Department of Trade and Industry announced the appointment of David Edmonds as the new Director General of Telecommunications, to take over from Don Cruickshank on 1 April 1998.

◆ The Government published its Green Paper Review of Utility Regulation.

◆ OFTEL's response to the European Commission on the Green Paper on the convergence of the telecommunications, media and information technology sectors, and the implications for regulation was published. In the response Don Cruickshank warned against a 'Euro Regulator' for the communications industry

◆ OFTEL's draft work programme for 1998/99 was published. This was the first year that OFTEL consulted publicly before drawing up its work programme. A public meeting was also held as part of its commitment to improving openess and accountability.

◆ OFTEL published its annual report for the year to 31 December 1997.

◆ The Director General announced he intended to stop the British Fax Directory calling whole ranges of phone numbers automatically in order to identify fax machines, which were then sent junk faxes.

◆ The statement Towa rds Better Telecoms for Customers was issued, showing that telecommunications customers were getting better deals and more choice.

## APRIL

◆ David Edmonds started work as Director General of Telecommunications.

◆ Following consultation, changes were made to the licences of One 2 One and Orange. The alteration meant that they would no longer have to provide airtime to mobile service providers. Details were set out in the statement Modification of the Licences of Orange and Mercury Personal Communications (MPCL).

◆ A set of draft regulations on new consumer protection measures was introduced. Details were set out in Identification of Operators with Significant Market Power for the Application of Detailed Rules under Purposes of the EC Voice Telephony and Universal Service Directive.

◆ After long public consultation, guidelines and licence changes were made as part of Europe-wide legislation to ensure fair competition in service provision. Details were contained in the statement Interconnection and Interoperability of Services over Telephony Networks.

## MAY

◆ The Independent Television Commission, the Office of Fair Trading and OFTEL established machinery to handle issues that cross the traditional boundaries between regulators in the field of communications.

◆ OFTEL's submission to the Monopolies and Mergers Commission inquiry into the Prices of Calls to Mobile Phones was published.

◆ OFTEL announced that the licence condition in the Telecommunications Services Licence is to be strengthened so as the clamp down on all companies that send out junk faxes or contract out their faxing to third parties.

## JUNE

◆ The Director General warned a company to stop making telesales calls to customers who do not want to receive them. Even after being asked by the complainant to stop making calls, the company concerned could give no assurances that they would not continue to do so.

## JULY

- The publicity campaign – the 'Big Number' – for the National Code and Number Change was launched.

- OFTEL agreed an extension until December for the MMC inquiry into the price of calling mobile phones.

- As part of the new national numbering scheme, OFTEL proposed that all freephone numbers will move to the 080 range. OFTEL issued a consultation document Freephone numbers: Options for the Future to discuss the most effective option of bringing freephone numbers to this range.

- OFTEL announced that it will collect and publish information every quarter on the volume of calls between the UK and abroad and the prices agreed between operators for carrying them. The development of the international calls market will be strictly watched to safeguard competition as the effects of liberalisation takes place.

- The consolation document Carrier Pre-Selection in the UK was published. It proposed that BT and Kingston customers can be connected to the telephone network by one operator, but can send their calls via a different operator if they want to.

- Following a warning in June, the company James E James was issued with a final enforcement order forbidding the company to call The Greek Taverna, which complained of nuisance telesales calls.

- The results of the review of Kingston Communications' licence were announced in the statement Review of the Telecommunications Act Licence of Kingston Communications (Hull) plc and Kingston upon Hull City Council. OFTEL proposed a number of measures to extend choice for the people and businesses of Hull.

## AUGUST

- The Director General called on telephone companies to safeguard consumers against misleading Premium Rate Services. In an open letter to the chief executives of all UK telecommunications companies, the Director General asked them to put consumers first when agreeing contracts for premium rate services.

- OFTEL announced in Determination of the Payphone Access Charge that BT must reduce its payphone access charge. OFTEL's investigations found that BT was passing on too many of its operating costs as part of call charge. OFTEL also published Determination of Competitiveness of Access to Indirect Access Operator Services from Payphones.

◆ OFTEL gave its support to the Telecoms Operator Forum, supported by 20 telecommunications companies, to beat the Year 2000 bug and ensure that the phone networks will not suffer when the date changes to 1 January 2000.

---

## SEPTEMBER

◆ OFTEL welcomed commitments by BT to ensure that the telesales staff marketing BT Click Internet services cannot access customer calling information. OFTEL launched an investigation following complaints that some BT sales staff were using customer information to identify regular Internet users. This appeared to contravene the Fair Trade Licence condition in BT's Licence.

◆ OFTEL's statement Provision of Directory Information Services and Products was published. It announced a package of new measures to improve directory services for consumers following a major review. More companies will be able to offer directory services so that consumers will be able to have more choice and possibly cheaper services. A Consumer Guide accompanied the statement.

◆ OFTEL published the statement Telecommunications Services for People with Disabilities, which unveiled a series of proposals aimed at giving people with disabilities easier access to the telecommunications network. The statement outlined a series of measures that telecommunications companies should put in place to ensure that people with disabilities have proper access to telecommunications services. A Consumer Guide accompanied the statement.

---

## OCTOBER

◆ Ionica plc was put into the hands of Administrators. OFTEL held discussions with the Administrators to ensure that there would be no interruption in service to Ionica's customers. The Administrators agreed to transfer customers to an alternative supplier or suppliers if a buyer is not found.

◆ OFTEL announced that BT's bundled discounts scheme for business appeared to be acceptable within the Fair Trading rules. OFTEL published the statement Tariffing Issues: Bundling of Inbound and Outbound Services.

---

## NOVEMBER

◆ OFTEL announced full details of its restructuring. The restructuring created a more flexible and better focused structure to enable OFTEL to respond more quickly to new challenges in the fast-moving communications world. A streamlined operations system is built around two directorates – Regulatory Policy and Compliance – backed by a Business Support Directorate.

◆ OFTEL published a consultation document Proposals for Publishing Information on Complaints Received by OFTEL which set out plans to publish information on the complaints it receives from customers about telecommunications companies and services. This information will help customers to be better informed when choosing phone suppliers and encourage telecommunications companies to solve the root cause of the complaints.

## DECEMBER

◆ OFTEL launched a consultation on how to ensure that consumers get access to information age services. The document Access to Bandwidth – Bringing Higher Bandwidth Services to the Consumer examined what steps were needed to ensure that families and small businesses are provided with innovative services such as high-speed Internet access and video on demand.

◆ The Director General announced that he intends to implement fully the recommendations made by the MMC following an investigation, made at the request of OFTEL, into the price of calls made to mobile phones. As a result, the costs of calls from a BT line to Vodafone or Cellnet mobile phones will fall by 25%.

◆ An agreement was reached between BT and the administrators of Ionica to ensure continuity of service to Ionica customers.

◆ OFTEL made an interim statement on its review of its investigation into Cable and Wireless Communications' (CWC) 999 operator service. OFTEL required CWC to provide a detailed timetable for the overhaul of its database that 999 operators use. CWC stated that this will be completed by March 1999.

◆ From 1 January 1999, mobile phone customers will be able to keep their old number when switching networks. The UK is the first country in the world to give customers this facility.

# A. **Working for Customers**

## Introduction

A.1   OFTEL's goal is to provide the best possible deal for the customer in terms of quality, choice and value for money. OFTEL believes that, wherever possible, effective competition provides the best way of securing lasting benefits for consumers.

A.2   OFTEL has five high-level objectives aimed at promoting competition in the telecommunications industry, while also protecting consumers (particularly those who are vulnerable or disadvantaged) where competition has yet to develop. These objectives are to:

- promote fair, efficient and sustainable network competition;
- promote fair, efficient and sustainable services competition;
- secure licence enforcement and fair trading;
- secure a fair distribution of the benefits of competition between different groups of customers;
- protect consumer interests, especially where effective competition is not yet fully developed.

A.3   These objectives enable consumers to protect their own interests by exercising choice wherever possible and prevent abuses of market power where effective competition is not yet available. The measure of success is whether consumers are satisfied with the range of products and services.

## Towards the best deal for customers – increasing choice

A.4   Telecommunications – from basic voice telephony to fax, mobile, Internet, and more advanced telecommunications services – increasingly underpin the economy and society of the UK. These communications markets are fast-moving, dynamic and converging, and are increasingly carrying text, images, and financial and other data in addition to voice messages.

### INCREASING VOLUMES

A.5   Revenue from the UK telecommunications market (including fixed and mobile networks and telecommunications equipment companies) grew by 7.2% between 1996/97 and 1997/98 from £22.2 billion to £23.8 billion. Telecommunications revenues account for some 2% of GDP. As the largest UK telecommunications company, BT has a declining share of these revenues – down by around 1% to 64% in the year to March 1998. BT's share of individual telecommunications markets in 1997/98 varies from around 87% of fixed telephone lines to under 40% of revenues from international business calls.

A.6 The volume of activity is increasing in fixed, mobile and other markets in terms of both the number of lines and the number of subscribers:

**Table 1:** Changes in telecommunications and related market sectors in numbers of lines or subscribers in 1998

|  | number of lines or subscribers (millions) | % increase over previous year (%) | Increase measured over year to: |
|---|---|---|---|
| Fixed | 32m lines | 4 | March 1998 |
| Mobile | 13m subscribers | 50 | Estimate December 1998 |
| Internet | c. 2.5m subscribers | c. 150 | Estimate December 1998 |
| Pay TV (satellite and cable) | 7m subscribers | 15 | Estimate August 1998 |

It is also increasing in terms of call minutes and other usage measures:

**Table 2:** Changes in volumes of use of telecommunications in 1998

|  | Volume of use | increase over previous year (%) | Increase measured over year to: |
|---|---|---|---|
| Fixed | 155 billion call minutes | 12 | March 1998 |
| Mobile | 10 billion call minutes | 40 | March 1998 |

A.7 More customers are using more networks and services. This creates an incentive for businesses to compete in these markets. Customers will benefit from competition in the telecommunications market as this should lead to better value for money through:

- expanding choice; leading to
- falling prices;
- improved quality of service.

A.8 Developments in each of these areas are described below.

EXPANDING CHOICE

A.9 Where customers have an effective choice of suppliers they are likely to obtain the benefits of competition. Choice has increased over the past year.

A.10 **Choice of fixed link telecommunications:** By October 1998, cable companies had laid cable past nearly 12 million households offering direct-to-the-home telecommunications connections. This represents a 15% increase in one year in the number of homes with access to cable telephony. Around 50% of households in the UK now have a choice of a cable operator to provide telecommunications services.

A.11 Take-up of cable telephone lines by residential customers was 3.4 million at October 1998, a 23% increase over October 1997. Cable companies are due to have passed 60% of households by the end of 2001.

A.12 Greater choice for residential and business customers has arisen from growth in the range and type of services provided by:

- ◆ long-distance and regional players
- ◆ indirect service providers
- ◆ fixed radio access suppliers.

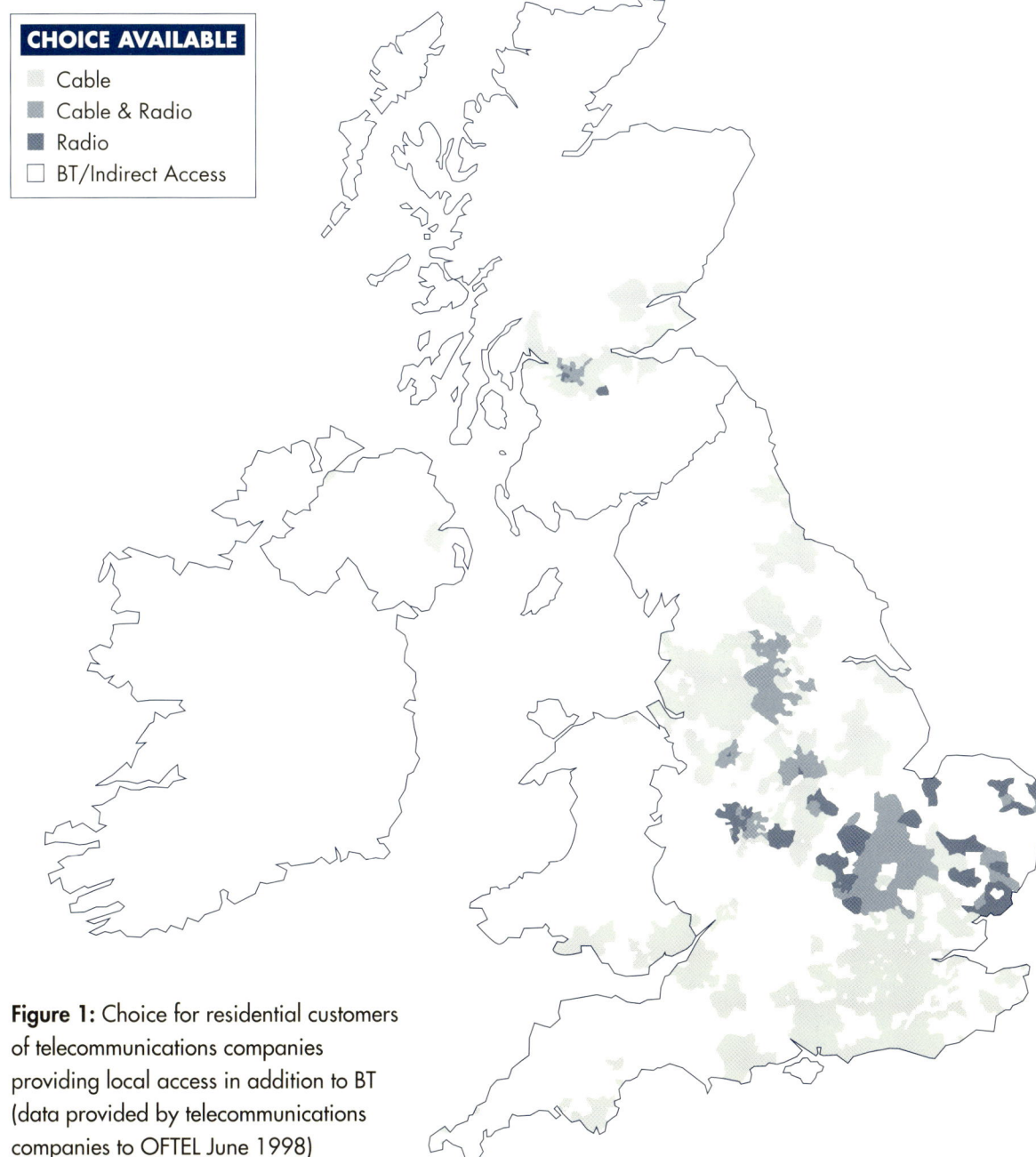

**CHOICE AVAILABLE**
Cable
Cable & Radio
Radio
BT/Indirect Access

**Figure 1:** Choice for residential customers of telecommunications companies providing local access in addition to BT (data provided by telecommunications companies to OFTEL June 1998)

A.13 The map shown in **Figure 1** highlights those areas where households have a choice of two or more telecommunications companies that provide direct connections to the home. However, those areas where residential customers only have a choice of a direct connection from BT also have a range of indirect access suppliers. Over 40 companies are providing indirect access services, mainly for national and international calls. To access a company's services, the customer dials a four-digit code before dialling the number they want.

A.14 **Choice of mobile telecommunications:** Mobile telecommunications services are provided by four network players. Between them these networks, had, in December 1998, some 13 million customers, an increase of 50% over the previous year. All four mobile networks claim UK population coverage of 96% or more. Cellnet also claimed an 85% *geographic* coverage level in 1998.

A.15 The two more recently established networks (Orange and One 2 One) had around 30% of total revenues for the period January to March 1998. This represents a considerable increase in choice from 1994 when the new mobile systems had only just started.

A.16 **Choice of Internet providers:** In 1998, the Internet was the service provided over telecommunications networks with the highest visibility for customers.

A.17 As Internet service providers do not have to operate under an individual licence, the number of subscribers is harder to estimate. Surveys towards the end of 1998 indicated around two million to three million residential and business subscribers in the UK.

A.18 Multi-user subscriptions (by companies and educational establishments) mean that the number of people who use the Internet is greater than those who subscribe to it. It has been estimated that in 1998 there were around 10 million users in the UK. The Internet has grown phenomenally over the last year, and most analysts suggest that the number of users has increased by well over 100%. Further evidence of growth in this area came with the recent announcement from BT that its network is now carrying more data traffic than voice traffic.

A.19 The choice of Internet service providers for customers is wide. There are several emerging mass market players – such as AOL, Compuserve, Demon and Dixon Freeserve – as well as many smaller niche players.

A.20 **Choice of pay TV suppliers:** This year has brought increased choices for customers in terms of broadcast services. As well as the 'free to air' channels (BBC1 and 2, ITV, Channel 4 and Channel 5), customers can now receive further TV channels through cable and satellite and terrestrial systems by paying a subscription or, in certain instances, on a 'pay per view' basis.

A.21 By August 1998 there were 6.9million satellite and cable households in the

UK (split 60:40 between satellite and cable). In the last quarter of 1998 digital broadcasting services were launched (by Sky Digital and On Digital); over time these are likely to supersede existing analogue broadcasting services. Access to these services will be via 'set top boxes' which will also be able to encompass traditional telecommunications connections and services.

A.22 Choice of suppliers in these markets is only just emerging, and further launches of digital broadcasting ventures are planned for 1999.

A.23 **Summary of choice:** The numbers of households and subscribers taking the various telecommunications services described above are shown in Figure 2. The different methods of delivering telecommunications service will increasingly be able to carry a wider range of overlapping services.

**Figure 2:** Main residential customer uses of telecommunications services

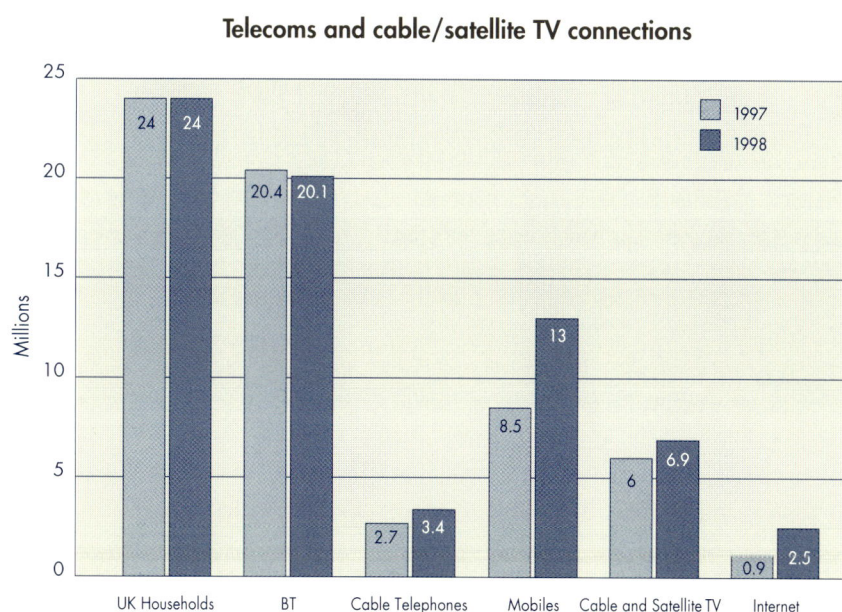

Telecoms and cable/satellite TV connections

## Price comparisons for residential customers

A.24 OFTEL is working with consumer groups and telecommunications companies to try to improve customers' opportunities to compare the prices offered by telecommunications companies. Following lengthy discussions with the industry during the first half of 1998, telecommunications pricing consultants funded by the main fixed link telecommunications companies are now developing a model to help residential customers to compare how much they would pay with different telecommunications companies.

A.25 Using a large sample of billing data provided by the telecommunications companies, the consultants have identified a range of customer profiles to reflect the different types of call patterns. The tariffs of telecommunications companies will be applied to these profiles to allow bills for different customer types to be compared.

***Customer profile x Telecommunication companies tariffs = Bills payable***

A.26 A number of key features have already emerged from the customer profile development work so far. The two critical elements, in order of importance, are:

- ◆ the proportion of local calls; and

- ◆ the proportion of daytime; weekday calls.

The following factors are also relevant:

- ◆ how often international calls are made;

- ◆ how often calls to mobiles are made;

- ◆ how often local rate calls are made, eg to 0345 numbers.

Further work is being undertaken to assess the influence of these factors.

A.27 Customers will select the customer profile that most closely matches their own calling pattern. The comparison model will then allow them to compare their current phone bill with the charges made by other telecommunications companies.

A.28 The consultants are due to complete their work on the model development by the end of March 1999. The aim is for the model to be developed by that time so that customers can successfully identify their call profile and the tariffs and discount schemes of the telecommunications companies can be taken into account in comparing bills.

A.29 Where this is the case, it should be feasible for regular price comparisons (say on a quarterly basis) to be put into the public domain, prepared and published by independent pricing consultants on behalf of the main fixed operators.

A.30 Customers will have the opportunity to be able to more easily compare prices. OFTEL is working with the fixed link industry and with consumer groups to make this happen.

## Retail price control

A.31 The current price control arrangements for BT's retail prices took effect on 1 August 1997. The major element of retail price control is a price cap formula of RPI-4.5% weighted to focus price reductions on the bottom 80% of BT's residential customers by spend. This means that BT has to reduce its prices in a way that reflects the calling patterns of lower spending customers (high proportion of spend on rental and local calls, lower proportion on national calls and a very low proportion on international calls).

PRICE CHANGES DURING 1998

A.32 Because of the price control BT was required to reduce its main prices to achieve revenue reductions of £44.3million in the price control year ending 31 July 1998. It achieved a reduction in revenue £45.1million in this period. The excess reduction (£0.8million) is allowed to be counted against the 1998/99 target. The target for the 1998/99 price control year is £20.4 million (including the carry-over of £0.8million).

A.33 The main price changes made as a result of price control in 1997/98 are set out below.

- In October 1997, BT reduced charges for national night-time and evening calls by 10%. The price per minute for these calls fell from 3.95 to 3.55 pence (excluding VAT). These price changes reduced BT's revenue by £11.8million.

- In January 1998, BT reduced charges for international calls. Calls to Japan at all times were reduced by between 12% (daytime) and 21% (weekend). These changes were in response to the growing competition on this route. Weekend calls to those European countries in Chargeband 1a, which include France and Germany, and to Chargeband 6 (Australia/New Zealand) were reduced by 1%. These price changes reduced BT's revenue by £0.5million.

- Also in January, BT reduced charges for national and regional weekend calls by 10%. The price per minute for these calls fell from 2.8 to 2.51 pence (excluding VAT). These changes reduced BT's revenue by £7.6million.

- In March, BT increased the quarterly discount for its Option 15 tariff – the reference tariff since July 1996 for price control purposes – from 10% of the customer's bill to 11%. In price control terms, the effect of this change was to reduce BT's revenue by £13.6million.

- In April BT, made its final set of price reductions for 1997/98. These consisted of a 10% reduction in the charges for local evening and night-time calls. These changes reduced BT's revenue by £11.7million.

**Figure 3:** Annual percentage change in the Retail Prices Index (RPI) for all items and for the telephone costs component (BT) in the UK.

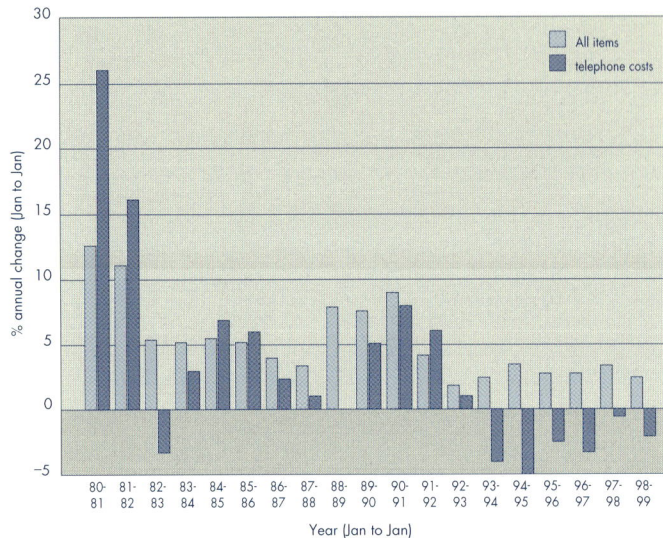

A.34 In November 1998, BT made the first set of changes for the 1998/99 price control year. The rental fee for Option 15 was reduced by 5.5% from £2.88 to £2.72 (excluding VAT); the standard quarterly exchange line rentals increased by £0.13 for residential customers to £22.78; and the Light User Scheme (LUS) was adjusted. Customers now receive a rental rebate of 1.274p for every 1p that their quarterly bill falls below £10.81. This meant that the maximum rebate for LUS customers fell from £13.93 to £13.77 (excluding VAT).

The net effect of these price changes was to reduce BT's revenue by £1.7m.

A.35 In 1998, BT changed the way it charged for calls on Christmas Day and New Year's Day. Instead of daytime calls being charged at night-time and evening rates, as in previous years, local, regional and national calls were subject to caps (after a certain call value is reached, no more is charged for that call) as set out below.

| Call Type | Local Daytime | Local Evening | Regional Daytime | Regional Evening | National Daytime | National Evening |
|---|---|---|---|---|---|---|
| Cap | 50p | 18.75p | 50p | 24.96p | 50p | 26.37p |

A.36 For international calls, daytime calls were charged at night-time and evening rates. These changes to Christmas Day and New Year's Day charges have reduced BT's revenue by £1.6million.

## PRIVATE CIRCUIT PRICES

A.37 In November, prices of inland analogue private circuits were increased on average by 3.7% – consistent with the increase in the Retail Prices Index (RPI). Prices of inland low capacity digital private circuits remained unchanged.

**Table 3:** Summary of BT's price changes controlled by Condition 24 of its licence (1984-1998)

| | PRICE CONTROL YEAR | | | | | | | | | | | | | |
|---|---|---|---|---|---|---|---|---|---|---|---|---|---|---|
| | 1984/ 1985 % | 1985/ 1986 % | 1986/ 1987 % | 1987/ 1988 % | 1988/ 1989 % | 1989/ 1990 % | 1990/ 1991 % | 1991/ 1992 % | 1992/ 1993 % | 1993/ 1994 % | 1994/ 1995 % | 1995/ 1996 % | 1996/ 1997 % | 1997/ 1998 % |
| RPI change in base period | 5.1 | 7.0 | 2.5 | 4.2 | 4.6 | 8.3 | 9.8 | 5.8 | 3.9 | 1.2 | 2.6 | 3.5 | 2.1 | 2.9 |
| RPI minus X[1] | 2.1 | 4.0 | −0.5 | 1.2 | 1.6 | 3.8 | 5.3 | −0.4 | −2.4 | −6.3 | −4.9 | −4.0 | −5.4 | −1.6 |
| Permitted increase[2] | 2.1 | 4.1 | −0.1 | 1.3 | 2.8 | 3.8 | 5.5 | −0.2 | −1.0 | −6.9 | −4.9 | −1.4 | −4.9 | −1.6 |
| Change in price of: | | | | | | | | | | | | | | |
| Exchange Line Rental[3] | | | | | | | | | | | | | | |
| residential (exclusive) | 7.1 | 8.5 | 3.7 | 0.0 | 0.0 | 10.0 | 11.6 | 7.8 | 5.9 | 3.2 | 4.6 | 3.7 | 3.6 | 0.0 |
| business (exclusive)[4] | 6.8 | 8.8 | 3.9 | 0.0 | 0.0 | 10.1 | 11.8 | 7.7 | 5.9 | 3.2 | 4.6 | 2.4 | 2.4 | n/a |
| wholesale lines | 6.8 | 8.8 | 3.9 | 0.0 | 0.0 | 10.1 | 11.8 | 10.8 | 8.8 | 6.2 | 7.6 | 0.0 | 0.0 | n/a |
| Connection Charges | | | | | | | | | | | | | | |
| residential[5] | n/a | n/a | n/a | n/a | n/a | n/a | n/a | n/a | n/a | −0.1 | −0.6 | 0.0 | 0.0 | 0.0 |
| business[5] | n/a | n/a | n/a | n/a | n/a | n/a | n/a | n/a | n/a | −24.6 | −11.3 | 0.0 | 0.0 | n/a |
| Change in effective price of: | | | | | | | | | | | | | | |
| Local Calls: | | | | | | | | | | | | | | |
| peak[6] | 6.8 | 6.4 | 18.9 | 0.0 | 0.0 | 0.0 | −4.5 | 3.5 | 0.0 | −22.6 | −8.7 | 0.0 | 0.0 | 0.0 |
| standard/daytime | 6.8 | 6.4 | 6.4 | 0.0 | 0.0 | 4.3 | −4.5 | 4.7 | 0.0 | 0.0 | −8.7 | 0.0 | 0.0 | 0.0 |
| cheap/evening & night | 6.8 | 6.4 | −3.6 | 0.0 | 0.0 | 3.7 | 10.1 | 4.6 | 0.0 | 0.0 | −1.2 | 0.0 | 0.0 | −6.6 |
| weekend[7] | 6.8 | 6.4 | −3.6 | 0.0 | 0.0 | 3.7 | 10.1 | 4.6 | 0.0 | 0.0 | −22.5 | 0.0 | 0.0 | 0.0 |
| Regional (a-rate) Calls: | | | | | | | | | | | | | | |
| peak[6] | 6.8 | 6.4 | 1.6 | 0.0 | 0.0 | 0.0 | −8.8 | 0.0 | 0.0 | −23.2 | −8.3 | 0.0 | −3.7 | 0.0 |
| standard | 6.8 | 18.3 | 1.1 | 0.0 | 0.0 | 0.0 | −9.0 | 0.0 | 0.0 | −0.2 | −8.3 | 0.0 | −3.7 | 0.0 |
| cheap | 23.1 | 6.4 | 2.7 | 0.0 | 0.0 | 3.6 | 6.0 | 4.9 | 0.0 | −0.2 | −2.5 | 0.0 | 0.0 | 0.0 |
| weekend cheap[7] | 23.1 | 6.4 | 2.7 | 0.0 | 0.0 | 3.6 | 6.0 | 4.9 | 0.0 | −9.0 | −10.5 | 0.0 | 0.0 | 9.4 |
| National (b1-rate) Calls: | | | | | | | | | | | | | | |
| peak[6] | −10.3 | −14.0 | −12.0 | 0.0 | 0.0 | 0.0 | −9.9 | 0.0 | 0.0 | −23.3 | −2.7 | 0.0 | −18.6 | 0.0 |
| standard | −10.2 | −13.8 | −12.0 | 0.0 | 0.0 | 0.0 | −10.0 | 0.0 | 0.0 | 0.0 | −2.7 | 0.0 | −18.6 | 0.0 |
| cheap | 6.8 | 6.4 | −12.0 | 0.0 | 0.0 | 0.0 | 7.1 | 4.9 | 0.0 | 0.0 | −6.9 | 0.0 | −19.8 | −9.8 |
| weekend cheap[7] | 6.8 | 6.4 | −12.0 | 0.0 | 0.0 | 0.0 | 7.1 | 4.9 | 0.0 | −41.1 | −8.7 | 0.0 | 0.0 | −9.8 |
| National (b-rate) Calls:[8] | | | | | | | | | | | | | | |
| peak[6] | −14.0 | −6.2 | −16.0 | 0.0 | 0.0 | 0.0 | −10.2 | 0.0 | 0.0 | −23.5 | −20.6 | 0.0 | −18.6 | 0.0 |
| standard | −13.9 | −4.9 | −17.0 | 0.0 | 0.0 | 0.0 | −10.1 | 0.0 | 0.0 | 0.0 | −20.6 | 0.0 | −18.6 | 0.0 |
| cheap | 6.8 | 6.4 | −6.2 | 0.0 | 0.0 | 0.0 | 7.0 | 4.9 | 0.0 | 0.0 | −28.4 | 0.0 | −19.8 | −9.8 |
| weekend cheap[7] | 6.8 | 6.4 | −6.2 | 0.0 | 0.0 | 0.0 | 7.0 | 4.9 | 0.0 | −55.2 | −7.6 | 0.0 | 0.0 | 0.0 |
| International Calls[5] | n/a | n/a | n/a | n/a | n/a | n/a | n/a | −9.8 | −4.7 | −5.5 | −4.4 | 0.0 | −18.2 | −0.3 |
| Directory Enquiries[5][9] | n/a | n/a | n/a | n/a | n/a | n/a | 4.4 | 0.0 | 0.0 | 0.0 | −43.5 | 0.9 | 0.0 | n/a[13] |
| Weighted average[10][11] | 2.0 | 3.7 | −0.3 | 0.0 | 0.0 | 3.5 | 5.3 | 2.1 | 1.0 | −6.9 | −7.3 | −1.0 | −4.3 | −0.7 |
| Overall Weighted average | 2.0 | 3.7 | −0.3 | 0.0 | 0.0 | 3.5 | 5.3 | −0.7 | −0.5 | −6.9 | −7.3 | −1.8 | −4.9 | −1.2 |

NOTES: Up to end of July 1998

1) 1984–1989, X=3: 1989–1991, X=4.5: 1991–1993, X=5.25: 1993–1997, X=7.5: 1997–2001, X=4.5.
2) After allowing for carryover of unused allowances from previous years.
3) Including basic telephone instrument in 1984 only.
4) November 1987: No increase in standard business rental, but rental for low loss exchange lines increased.
5) Each of these uses the RPI figure from the month prior to its inclusion in the basket as the RPI base for calculating the cumulative change in its prices in real terms: July 1993 RPI as a base for connection charges. July 1991 RPI as a base for international calls and March 1991 RPI as a base for directory enquiries.
6) The 'Peak' rate amalgamated with 'Standard' to become 'Daytime' in March 1994.
7) 'Weekend' regional/national and local calls were charged at cheap rate until December 1993 and June 1995 respectively. (The international 'Weekend' rate was introduced in September 1996)
8) In 1986 and again in 1989, routes were transformed from 'b' to 'b1'. The weighted averages take account of this. In September 1994 the 'b' rate was eliminated.
9) The 1990/91 figure is directory enquiry revenue as a percentage of total regulated revenue when charges were introduced: it is not included in the cumulative change figure.
10) Including services not identified above, in particular shared exchange lines, linklines, midnight lines, low loss lines and low user schemes. Linklines, midnight lines and low loss lines are business services and therefore were no longer in the basket from 1 August 1997.
11) September 1989: Includes the effect of a reduction in the number of concessionary days: 1990/91: In the basket submission this figure looks like it should be 0.9% because they took off DQ effects to look at other necessary changes.
12) From 1997/98 onwards the price control basket consists of revenues from the lowest 80% of residential customers only.
13) Directory Enquiries was taken out of the price control basket on 1 August 1997.
n/a Not Applicable – not included in the basket of controlled services.
The price control year runs from 1 August until the following 31st July. In the following price control years, the price changes only took place in the months shown.

| | | |
|---|---|---|
| 1984 – 1985 November 1984 | 1987 – 1988 November 1987 | 1990 – 1991 September 1990 and April 1991 |
| 1985 – 1986 November 1985 | 1988 – 1989 November 1988 | 1991 – 1992 September 1991 |
| 1986 – 1987 November 1986 | 1989 – 1990 September 1989 | 1992 – 1993 January 1993 and July 1993 |

**Table 4:** Summary of BT private circuit prices controlled by Condition 24 B of its licence (1989 -1998)

| | PRICE CONTROL YEAR | | | | | | | | | |
|---|---|---|---|---|---|---|---|---|---|---|
| | 1989/ 1990 % | 1990/ 1991 % | 1991/ 1992 % | 1992/ 1993 % | 1993/ 1994 % | 1994/ 1995 % | 1995/ 1996 % | 1996/ 1997 % | 1997/ 1998 % | 1998/ 1999 % |
| RPI change in base period | 11.30[1] | 9.80 | 5.80 | 3.90 | 1.22 | 2.62 | 3.52 | 2.14 | 2.94 | 3.75 |
| Permitted increases[2] inland digital | | | | | | 5.28 | 9.14 | 11.50 | | |
| inland analogue | 11.30 | 9.80 | 7.80 | 4.30 | 1.22[3] | 2.63 | 3.79 | 2.44 | 2.94 | 3.75 |
| international | | | | | | 13.07 | 18.13 | 19.25 | | |
| **Change in the price of private circuits:** **Inland Digital** **MegaStream** connection | 2.90 | −2.40 | −15.70 | −5.90 | −15.90 | 0.00 | −4.39 | −0.04 | n/a | n/a |
| rental | 21.70 | −3.70 | −0.10 | −4.40 | −2.00 | −0.94 | −0.13 | −0.21 | n/a | n/a |
| KiloStream connection | 0.00 | 9.30 | 9.80 | 0.00 | 0.00 | 0.00 | 0.00 | 0.00 | 0.00 | 0.00 |
| rental | 0.00 | −0.90 | −1.70 | 0.00 | 0.00 | −0.01 | 0.00 | 0.00 | 0.06 | 0.00 |
| Inland Digital Total[5] | n/a | −1.60 | −1.60 | −2.10 | −1.44 | −0.34 | −0.22 | −0.07 | −0.06 | 0.00 |
| **Inland Analogue** connection | 13.80 | 14.70 | 28.10 | 3.90 | 2.50 | 0.93 | 2.05 | 1.97 | 2.19 | 1.09 |
| rental | 11.90 | 11.10 | 10.60 | 3.80 | 1.10 | 2.55 | 3.69 | 2.14 | 3.00 | 3.93 |
| Inland Analogue Total | n/a | 11.60 | 12.90 | 3.80 | 1.21 | 2.36 | 3.48 | 2.12 | 2.93 | 3.73 |
| International Analogue | n/a | n/a | 2.00 | 6.00 | 2.20 | 4.43 | 4.93 | 3.40 | 0.00 | 0.00 |
| International Digital | n/a | n/a | −1.10 | 0.00 | −14.40 | −3.92 | 0.00 | 0.00 | 0.00 | 0.00 |
| International Total | n/a | n/a | 0.50 | 2.40 | −9.23 | −1.54 | 1.02 | 0.39 | 0.00 | 0.00 |
| Weighted Average | 11.30 | 7.80 | 7.40 | 1.80 | −0.90 | 0.88 | 1.54 | 0.73 | 1.57 | 1.76 |
| RPI Index all items[4] | 126.8 | 133.8 | 138.8 | 140.7 | 144.0 | 149.1 | 152.4 | 157.5 | 159.5 | 163.4 |

Until end of 1997/98 Price Control

NOTES:
1) The price constraint for the first year was the increase in RPI over 16 months.
2) After allowing for carryover of unused allowances from previous years.
3) Since August 1993, there have been three seperate private circuit baskets each with overall price rises limited to a maximum increase of RPI.
4) Base: Jan '87=100. The RPI values shown are the July figures at the end of the relevant price control year. The 1996/97 figure is based on RPI data to January 1998 only. July 1989 (115.5) is used as the RPI base for cumulative price changes in real terms since private circuit price control began..
5) From 1 August 1997, high capacity (over 64 kbit/s) digital circuits were taken out of the inland digital basket. The international basket was removed from price control although individual international circuits remained constrained by a safeguard cap of RPI. There remain 2 general private circuit baskets: Inland Analogue and Inland Low Capacity Digital, both of which are constrained by an increase of no more than RPI.
n/a  Not Available

**Table 5:** Summary of BT Private circuit prices controlled by Condition 24B of its licence (1998/99)

| Since start of Control in August 1997[1] | 1997/98 | 1998/99 |
|---|---|---|
| RPI change in base period | 2.94% | .75% |
| **Permitted increases:** | | |
| Inland Low Capacity Digital | 2.94% | 3.75% |
| Inland Analogue | 2.94% | 3.75% |
| **CHANGE IN THE PRICE OF PRIVATE CIRCUITS:** | | |
| **Inland Low Capacity Digital** | | |
| KiloStream | | |
| Connection | 0.00% | 0.00% |
| Rental | -0.06% | 0.00% |
| **Inland Digital Total** | -0.06% | 0.00% |
| Inland Analogue | | |
| Connection | 2.19% | 1.09% |
| Rental | 3.00% | 3.93% |
| **Inland Analogue Total** | 2.93% | 3.73% |
| **Weighted Average** | 1.57% | 1.76% |

Notes :
(1) From 1 August 1997, high capacity (over 64 kbit/s) digital circuits were taken out of the digital basket. The international basket was removed from price control although individual international circuits remained constrained by a safeguard cap of RPI. There remain two general private circuit baskets: Inland Low Capacity Digital and Inland Analogue, both of which are constrained by an increase of no more than RPI.

**Source:** OFTEL

## Prices of calls to mobiles

A.38 Following concerns expressed by consumers that the prices of calls to mobiles were excessive, OFTEL began an investigation into the charges made by mobile operators for terminating calls and BT's added costs and profit margin. As a result of the investigation, OFTEL concluded that the prices charged were too high in relation to cost.

A.39 In March 1998, the Director General asked the Monopolies and Mergers Commission (MMC) to investigate whether the level of charges were in the public interest. He also referred the matter of Cellnet's and Vodafone's practice of charging for unanswered or diverted calls.

A.40 The MMC reported in December 1998. Its key conclusions were that:

♦ the interconnection charges made by Cellnet and Vodafone were too high in relation to cost;

◆ BT's retention was excessive;

◆ the practice of charging for unanswered calls should stop; and

◆ these matters acted against the public interest.

A.41 The MMC proposed that the charges be reduced by an average 25% for the year 1999/2000 and be subject to price control for the following two years of RPI-9% (in the case of the mobile operators) and RPI-7% (in the case of BT). The costs of unanswered calls should be recovered from successful calls, and this has been factored into the above figures.

A.42 The Director General has accepted the MMC's recommendations and has implemented them fully. It is estimated that the savings for consumers will be more than £1billion over the three years of the price control.

## Quality of service

A.43 As competition develops, price is not the only basis on which telecommunications companies compete. Customers will also get a better deal where telecommunications suppliers compete on the basis of the quality of service provided and the range of services available.

A.44 For fixed link services, the main telecommunications companies are reporting their quality of service in a comparable way so that customers can take quality factors into account when making purchasing decisions. Those telecommunications companies that reported in 1998 across the majority of comparable quality of service measures, as defined and agreed by industry and consumer groups, accounted for 98% of residential and 93% of business market retail revenues.

A.45 Mobile operators do not currently report quality of service information on a comparable basis. In the absence of such data, OFTEL commissioned a one-off illustrative survey of calls made from mobile phones on the different networks. The success rate varied more widely between networks on calls made from selected rail routes than from the three cities surveyed (London, Cardiff and Edinburgh). The overall call failure rate was 1 in 5 on the rail routes and 1 in 20 in the cities.

A.46 A range of measures of Internet quality of service exist and are published in magazines and on the Internet itself. However no industry 'standard' measures widely recognised by consumers have yet emerged. Nor have industry standards for quality of service for pay TV services.

## Comparable performance indicators

A.47 OFTEL has continued to support the industry's efforts to produce and publish comparable performance indicators for residential and business telecommunications services. These give consumers a real opportunity to make direct comparisons between the quality of service provided by the different operators and therefore to make an informed choice.

A.48  During 1998 more operators participated in the exercise. Some 14 operators published figures for the residential report in October, while 22 contributed to the business report.

A.49  In October Comparable Performance Indicators were published on the world wide web (http://www/telecommunications company-cpi.org.uk).

## Price trends

A.50  Competition, and price controls where competition is not fully effective, have driven prices down in real terms. Between 1984 and 1998 prices for the main fixed link BT services fell in real terms by about 50%. Retail and wholesale prices continue to be controlled by price arrangements. In 1999, OFTEL will begin the process of reviewing the need for further controls.

A.51  Prices for mobile services have fallen on average, across customer types, by 17% in real terms since 1997 and by 70% since 1990.

A.52  Trend information in Internet services and converging broadcasting services is less easy to calculate because of the wide range of tariff types and the rapid changes in the underlying services they relate to. For example, recent estimates have suggested that Freeserve now has more than 1 million subscribers.

## Consumer complaints and enquiries

A.53  The Director General has a statutory duty to consider complaints and enquiries made to him about telecommunications services. This public service is provided, on the Director General's behalf, by OFTEL's Consumer Representation Section.

A.54  In addition, the Northern Ireland Advisory Committee on Telecommunications, the Scottish Advisory Committee on Telecommunications, and the Welsh Advisory Committee on Telecommunications also deal on the Director General's behalf with complaints and enquiries from consumers in their respective countries. Reports by these committees can be found in Part Three of this report.

A.55  Customer complaints and enquiries received by OFTEL about telecommunications companies and others give an overview of key aspects of market developments. **The total number of complaints and enquiries continues to increase:**

| Year | 1994 | 1996 | 1998 |
|---|---|---|---|
| Numbers of complaints and queries | 30 800 | 36 100 | 50 600 |

A.56  During 1998, 50,000 people contacted OFTEL for help and advice, an increase of around 19% on 1997. The number of complaints showed a corresponding rise. Enquires doubled compared with 1997.

A.57 The upward trend shows that customers are now more aware of choice and are more demanding and critical of the services they receive. The changing subject matter of complaints also indicates developments in the use of networks. Customer complaints are moving away from concerns about the basic reliability of fixed networks towards services delivered over networks and towards new types of networks. Unsolicited fax messages were the subject of more complaints to OFTEL during 1998 than any other subject. The number of complaints about Internet services also began to increase substantially during 1998, reflecting the increase in activity in this sector and confirming the dynamic nature of the telecommunications market.

A.58 OFTEL received 2150 contacts from consumers raising questions, queries and information requests about its activities. The main area of interest from consumers related to OFTEL's numbering policy.

A.59 OFTEL maintained its policy of encouraging network operators and service providers to resolve consumer disputes directly with their customers. When disputes cannot be resolved in this way, customers have the option of coming back to OFTEL for further assistance. In many instances (in which OFTEL has no powers to act), OFTEL uses a good-offices role in an endeavour to resolve the dispute.

A.60 During the year OFTEL continued to encourage network operators and service providers to raise service standards, such as answering letters from customers promptly, improving the quality of replies and addressing complaints about difficulties in calling customer services. While there were some overall improvements in the cable sector – where company mergers had led to problems in maintaining service standards – OFTEL was disappointed with the level of consumer complaints it continued to receive about service standards. One reason for the high volume of complaints appears to be related to increased consumer demand for mobile services, which has required some companies to recruit more customer facing staff.

A.61 Consumer concern about privacy issues escalated during the year. This was largely because of a significant increase in complaints (over 9% of the total complaints received for the year) to OFTEL from consumers fed up with receiving junk fax messages.

A.62 OFTEL also received a large number of complaints from consumers who felt that the contracts they had signed for telecommunications service were unfair in some way. Generally these related to the conditions in mobile service provider contracts covering termination periods or fees associated with terminating an agreement. The Office of Fair Trading's Unfair Contracts Unit has been instrumental in a number of companies revising their contract conditions. OFTEL hopes that it will therefore see a decrease in this type of complaint. OFTEL will also have the option of exercising its powers under new EC legislation if problems persist.

A.63 In February 1998 OFTEL'S *Improving Accountability* statement set out actions for the publication of consumer complaint/enquiry data, with the aim of providing greater incentive for telecommunications companies to address the cause of complaints and to improve information available to consumers. This will help consumers make better informed decisions about their choice of service. The published data would show a Top 10 complaints table and a Top 10 companies table and was intended to be published in September. Some telecommunications companies raised concerns regarding the proposed publication. OFTEL agreed to review the approach of the publication and to consult with the telecommunications industry and consumers and their representative organisations over the most valuable way of presenting the data. The consultation document *Proposals for Publishing Information on Complaints Received by OFTEL* was published in November 1998. It is intended that OFTEL will publish complaints data in May 1999.

**Table 6:** A breakdown of issues raised by consumers received by OFTEL [and Consumer Communications for England]

| Category | Complaints | | Enquiries | |
|---|---|---|---|---|
| | **1998** | **1997** | **1998** | **1997** |
| Disputed Bills | 2600 | 2900 | 50 | 50 |
| Other problems with bills | 3100 | 2600 | 50 | 50 |
| Bill payment problems | 3600 | 3050 | 100 | 100 |
| Charges | 3000 | 2200 | 300 | 200 |
| Installations | 2400 | 2000 | 100 | 100 |
| Numbering | 950 | n/a | 3250 | n/a |
| Payphones | 300 | 300 | 50 | 50 |
| Phonebooks | 350 | 250 | 50 | 50 |
| Privacy | 5850 | 2250 | 400 | 400 |
| Quality of customer service | 6800 | 6750 | 150 | 150 |
| Quality of telecommunications service | 2050 | 2050 | 150 | 150 |
| Rental | 600 | 1100 | 50 | 50 |
| Repair service | 2400 | 1950 | 0 | 50 |
| Network and discount services | 1050 | 1600 | 50 | 100 |
| General information request | 0 | 700 | 5450 | 2500 |
| Miscellaneous | 7000 | 5400 | 2900 | 2600 |
| | **42050** | **35100** | **13100** | **6600** |

Note 1: numbering is a new category for 1998; previously issues related to numbering were in the miscellaneous category
Note 2: figures rounded to nearest 50

**Figure 4:** Who the complaints were about.

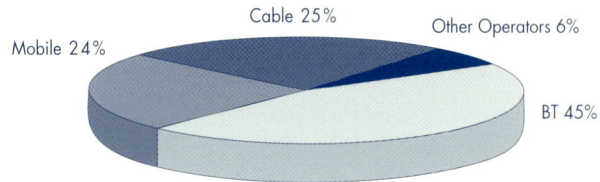

Cable 25%  Other Operators 6%

Mobile 24%

BT 45%

Note: these figures relate to 76% of issues raised; the other 24% did not concern individual telephone companies

## Failure of Ionica plc

A.64 OFTEL was concerned when it learned of the first failure of a network operator, Ionica plc, a licensed public telecommunications operator providing a telephony service using fixed radio links.

A.65 In early autumn, Ionica informed OFTEL that it would have to appoint administrators. From that point OFTEL worked with the Administrators and latterly with BT and cable companies to protect customers' interests. OFTEL's prime concern was to ensure continuity of supply of a telephone service to all Ionica customers.

A.66 When the Administrator reached the decision to cease trading, OFTEL ensured that customers were re-assured that a process was in place to provide for orderly transfer of the provision of telephony services to another operator. The Administrator was committed to providing no break in service and engaged BT to manage the orderly transfer of service to BT or a cable company where one was available. Customers were given contact numbers for BT and cable companies to enable them to decide which company they wished to move to.

A.67 OFTEL also ensured that the Administrator released the names and addresses of all Ionica customers to cable companies to enable these companies to contact customers directly to offer a cable service. We understand that cable companies did use this information to contact Ionica customers.

A.68 As the Ionica network will cease to exist, the normal system, whereby customers can retain their telephone numbers when switching from one telephony supplier to another, will not operate, other than for those customers who retained a BT number when they switched from BT to Ionica. OFTEL is encouraged that over half of Ionica's customers were able to retain their numbers on this basis.

A.69 OFTEL was particularly concerned about the impact on business customers of the loss of an advertised telephone number. To enable a solution to be found, OFTEL reallocated telephone numbers held by Ionica to BT. The Administrator agreed that an intercept telephone answering machine message could be placed on Ionica lines to advise calling parties of the changed number prior to BT providing a Changed Number Announcement (CAN) or, for business lines, a Remote Call Forwarding (RCF) option when the Ionica network is switched off. BT will return the Ionica number blocks to OFTEL when customers no longer require CAN or RCF on the BT exchanges.

A.70  OFTEL kept closely in touch with the Administrator and telecommunications operators to facilitate a smooth transfer from Ionica to BT or to alternative operators. The Ionica network ceased operations on 28 February 1999.

## Opportunities for customers to get more from their phone

A.71  Research showing that customers could take greater advantage of new, advanced telecommunications services was published in July 1998 by consultants commissioned by OFTEL.

A.72  The survey of over 1000 business and residential customers and 26 telecommunications companies was designed to find how many customers knew about or used 35 'new' telecommunications services such as call waiting, the Internet and voice mail.

A.73  The results showed that, even though many customers are aware of new services, as yet few are taking advantage of them. For example, 84% of residential customers are aware that call waiting services exist, but only 16% use them.

A.74  This research will help OFTEL, telecommunications operators and consumers understand how the UK market is developing. For example, are customers getting the new innovative services they want and, in some cases, need? As a first step, clearer information from telecommunications companies will help customers be more informed buyers.

A.75  A report containing the research findings, *Advanced Telecommunications Services: Awareness, Take Up and Availability in the UK* was published by National Economic Research Associates (NERA). It is also available on NERA's website at http://www.nera.com/uk/papers.

A.76  OFTEL will review this research in 1999 to assess how much change has taken place.

## Payphones

A.77  In February, OFTEL published a consultative document that addressed a number of consumer concerns relating to the provision of public payphone services. *A Better Deal for Payphone Users* invited views on which services operators should be obliged to make available from their payphones and which should be left to their discretion. There is a balance to be struck – too much regulation could discourage competitive payphone provision, yet too little could leave users vulnerable. OFTEL put forward a view that there could be an increase in the obligations relating to those payphones in more public places which consumers expect to provide the full range of services.

A.78 The consultative document also addressed the issue of unauthorised advertising in public payphones, principally by prostitutes. A proposal from BT was presented which would allow it to bar access to any telephone numbers advertised in that way. OFTEL expressed the view that, if a consensus of opinion emerged on these issues, it would be prepared to put forward the necessary formal proposals for changes to the operators' licences.

A.79 The consultation exercise attracted a great deal of interest. However, OFTEL delayed publishing a response until 1999 pending expected policy announcements by the Home Office on unauthorised advertising.

## Telecommunications services for people with disabilities

A.80 In February, OFTEL launched a comprehensive consultation on the provision of telecommunications services for people with disabilities. This was followed up in September by a statement which outlined a series of measures that all the major telecommunications companies ought to implement in order to ensure that people with disabilities have proper access to the sorts of telecommunications services that the rest of the community take for granted.

A.81 This work was done in close co-operation with the Department of Trade and Industry (DTI), which has a responsibility to draft Regulations in this area in order to implement EC obligations. The DTI will be consulting on the final shape of the Regulations in 1999.

A.82 OFTEL's proposed obligations for the main telecommunications operators includes:

♦ widely publicising services for people with disabilities in appropriate ways;

♦ consulting interested groups on the needs of people with disabilities when new services and products are being developed;

♦ providing a free directory information service for people who cannot use a telephone directory;

♦ making calls cheaper for users of textphones to compensate for the fact that calls take longer when using textphones;

♦ making a text relay service available so that textphone users can call people who do not have a textphone;

♦ making it easier for textphone users to call 999;

- providing a priority fault repair service for people with disabilities who rely on the telephone;

- offering a special service for people with disabilities who wish to nominate a friend or relative to deal with their telephone bills etc;

- presenting, on request, bills and contractual information for people with impaired vision in Braille or large print or on computer disk;

- ensuring that most public phone boxes are reasonably accessible by wheelchair users, are hearing aid-compatible and have volume amplification;

- ensuring that a reasonable number of public call boxes are provided that are fully accessible by wheelchair and have textphone capabilities.

A.83 OFTEL does not have the power under the Telecommunications Act to address the problem that the cost of textphones and similar equipment prevents many speech-and hearing-impaired people from using the telecommunications network fully. OFTEL welcomed the DTI's commitment to look at this problem further.

## Emergency service calls

A.84 OFTEL continued its role as an observer on the Home Office organised '999' Liaison Committee, which provides a forum for the emergency authorities and telecommunications companies to identify and resolve issues regarding the emergency calls service. Issues considered by the Committee during 1998 included:

- readiness for the millennium date change;

- the ability to make an emergency call via an alternative Mobile Network Operator if a subscriber is outside the coverage area of their own Network Operator;

- routing of calls to the emergency services over virtual private networks;

- the connection of 112 emergency calls, in line with European directives;

- the returning of silent mobile calls to the emergency services;

- the availability of mobile subscriber information.

**Table 7:** Emergency call performance statistics for 1998

| Operator | Number of calls taken (millions) | % answered within 5 secs | % answered within 15 secs | Average time taken to answer a call |
|----------|----------------------------------|--------------------------|---------------------------|-------------------------------------|
| BT | 19.7 | 96.1 | 99.7 | n/a |
| CWC | 3.4 | 94.1 | 100.0 | 0.88 |
| Kingston | 0.2 | n/a | 99.97 | 1.06 |

## Directory information

A.85 In September, OFTEL published its statement *Directory Information Services and Products*. This set out a series of measures designed to:

- ◆ address the privacy concerns of residential consumers regarding the way their directory information is used;

- ◆ ensure that consumers have access to more comprehensive directory services and products;

- ◆ improve the quality, variety and choice of directory information services.

### PRIVACY CONCERNS

A.86 From 1999 consumers will have the right to choose how they are listed in a phone book, electronic directory or directory enquiry service. They will be able to choose:

- ◆ not to have an entry;

- ◆ not to have any reference to their gender;

- ◆ to have only part of their address listed.

A.87 OFTEL has also worked closely with the Data Protection Registrar to produce an enforceable Code of Practice on the use of directory information. This sets out what can and cannot be done with directory information. For example, it does not allow reverse searching where a telephone number is used to find an address.

### ACCESSING COMPREHENSIVE SERVICES

A.88 All telecommunications companies and service providers now have to pass directory information that they hold about their consumers to any telecommunications company that asks for it. This will enable all telecommunications companies to produce phone books and offer a directory enquiry service containing everyone's number. The telecommunications companies will be subject to the Code of Practice on the use of Directory Information.

### FAIR AND EFFECTIVE COMPETITION

A.89 At the beginning of 1999 BT will have to give organisations other than telecommunications companies access to the directory information that it holds. This is to enable these other organisations to offer competing directory enquiry services and directory products. These organisations will be subject to the Code of Practice on the use of Directory Information.

## Utility review

A.90 In March, the Government published its Green Paper *A Fair Deal for Consumers: Modernising the Framework for Utility Regulation.* This document was the result of extensive consultations during 1997 to meet the Government's manifesto commitment for a fundamental review of the way in which the utilities (water, electricity, gas and, for these purposes, telecommunications) are regulated.

A.91 OFTEL warmly welcomed the review, which looks to reinforce the need to place the interests of consumers at the heart of regulation. OFTEL also particularly welcomed the emphasis on the need for transparency and accountability in regulation.

A.92 During the year OFTEL participated in and influenced the course of the public debate. DTI went on to publish a White Paper, which confirmed the general thrust of the proposals, and specific consultations on its idea of independent Consumer Councils for each of the utilities.

A.93 OFTEL looks forward to the development of these proposals in 1999 and to the eventual drafting of a Bill. The changes proposed will, in some respects, be significant for OFTEL; the setting up of a Telecommunications Consumer Panel will make an enormous difference to the way in which OFTEL works. In other respects, many of the changes reflect the direction in which OFTEL has been taking telecommunications regulation in recent years and will be a natural development of OFTEL's ongoing efforts to address the needs of consumers.

# B. **Fostering Competition and Compliance**

## Introduction

B.1    The year 1998 saw a significant development in the nature and focus of OFTEL's work as it prepared for a new role as both a Regulator and a Competition Authority.

B.2    A major development was the review of how OFTEL should organise itself to deal with this new environment. This led to the creation of a new Compliance Directorate. This directorate took over all work dealing with competition and fair trading matters and assumed responsibility for all licence enforcement and competition and compliance activity previously spread across OFTEL. The Customer Representation Section was added, since analysis of customer complaints helps to identify wider compliance concerns.

B.3    In further preparation for the Competition Act, OFTEL offered to work with companies developing their own Compliance Programmes. Telecommunications operators have welcomed the idea of an Industry Forum. This will follow the consultation on Competition Act guidelines for the telecommunications industry early in 1999. Part of the compliance process has been to encourage companies to identify their own potential compliance problems and discuss plans for remedial action. The transition from detailed regulation to competition as the means of ensuring the best quality and value for money for customers can best be brought about by encouraging a compliance culture within the telecommunications industry.

B.4    OFTEL has developed the use of and interpretation of the Fair Trading Condition, introduced into licences in 1997, based on Articles 85 and 86 of the Treaty of Rome. These are also the basis of the new 1998 Competition Act. This has helped both companies complained about and those making competition complaints to understand the changes the new legislation requires and how compliance underpins this requirement.

B.5    This approach has increasingly led to OFTEL's earlier involvement in potential anti-competitive behaviour. Telecommunications operators have been able to understand OFTEL's views before taking actions that OFTEL believes could distort the market and have therefore modified their proposals. This is a better outcome for consumers than action taken by OFTEL after the event to remedy anti-competitive behaviour.

B.6    OFTEL has continued to consult interested parties. In a fast-moving industry, this puts pressure on all concerned if pre-emptive action is to be taken. OFTEL expects this development to continue as markets become more competitive and companies wish to be increasingly innovative in the products and services they offer.

B.7    Growing experience in the applications of the Fair Trading Condition has proved beneficial in developing the new regime. OFTEL played a key role in the

Concurrency Working Group, comprising the regulators and the Office of Fair Trading (OFT), and with other Government Departments in the development of the Competition Bill and, more recently, in implementation issues and the production of guidelines. This group has proved so useful that it will continue to assist in the development of the unified approach that is an essential element for the successful exercise of the concurrent powers under the Competition Act held by the Director Generals of the industry regulatory bodies and the Director General of Fair Trading.

B.8    As reported in the 1997 annual report, OFTEL's effectiveness in addressing competition complaints was the subject of an extensive examination by the National Audit Office (NAO). In April 1998, the NAO published its report on *Countering Anti-Competitive Behaviour in the Telecommunications Industry*. OFTEL was encouraged by the report's findings, in particular the recognition that it now acts more quickly in pursuing competition investigations. Subsequently, in June the Public Accounts Committee (PAC) examined the NAO report and took evidence from the Director General. The Director General has accepted all the recommendations in the NAO report and the conclusions that emerged from the PAC hearing.

B.9    Throughout 1998, OFTEL continued to look at ways of improving its performance in case handling. The early part of the year saw the introduction of a Casework Management Information System (CMIS) to assist management and case officers to monitor and track case progress. Excluding individual consumer complaints, all complaints have now been brought into CMIS and are now subject to casework targets. This resulted in a slight increase in the total number of cases over six months old.

B.10   CMIS provides case clearance details and is used by OFTEL to measure performance against targets. OFTEL aims to complete all preliminary enquiries within 30 working days. During 1998 OFTEL improved the clearance rate to 90% from 86% in 1997. OFTEL continues to strive towards meeting the ambitious 100% target. In 1998 the average length of a preliminary enquiry increased slightly from 4.2 to 4.47 weeks.

B.11   Following the NAO report, OFTEL tested revised targets for full investigations – to complete 75% of all investigations within three months and 100% within six months without any adverse effect on quality. Only 31% were concluded within three months. However 78% were concluded within six months; this exceeds the long-standing 75% clearance target. At the end of 1998 only five working cases were over six months old.

B.12   An important development following the NAO report in April 1998 and in preparation for the new Competition Act was the establishment of a review of the efficiency and effectiveness of the casework and compliance procedures in use across OFTEL. Quality monitoring and targets were key linked issues in the review.

OFTEL is aiming for good-quality casework and stretching but achievable targets. While reverting to its original headline targets, OFTEL has retained the new three month clearance target for less complex cases and is working towards increasing the percentage of cases settled within six months.

B.13 OFTEL's on-going work continues to develop as new markets grow and emerge and mergers, acquisitions and joint ventures alter the structure of the industry. Late in 1998, the proposed BT/AT&T joint venture absorbed, and continues to absorb, considerable resources. This is only one of 35 significant transactions (20 in 1997) on which OFTEL made assessments and gave advice to the UK and EU authorities.

## Compliance investigations

B.14 OFTEL has the responsibility for ensuring that telecommunications operators comply with the conditions of their licences, which are granted by the Secretary of State for Trade and Industry. It conducts investigations into breaches of licence conditions, including those related to consumer issues such as billing and unsolicited faxing, and those breaches involving competition issues such as undue preference or undue discrimination, and abuse of market power. These are the result of external complaints from other licensed operators, independent service providers, equipment suppliers, large business customers and consumers. OFTEL's other source of cases is its own-initiative investigations into potential policy and generic competition issues. It also carries out examinations of specific proposals relating to price changes, affinity deals and service trials that may affect competition.

B.15 In 1998, there was a large rise in the number of complaints to OFTEL about unsolicited faxing and calling. Some of these resulted in the issue of orders against originating companies. However, the present regulatory regime has proved ill-suited to deal with this issue. The implementation of the Telecommunications (Data Protection and Privacy (Direct Marketing) Regulations 1998 on 1 May 1999 will introduce a more effective control mechanism for dealing with unsolicited direct-marketing calls and faxes. Enforcement of the Regulations will be the responsibility of the Data Protection Registrar.

B.16 OFTEL adopts a two-stage investigation process in respect of compliance complaints. A preliminary phase determines whether there is a case to answer and whether to proceed to a full investigation. The investigation phase includes information collection, analysis and assessment to decide whether there has been a breach of licence and/or any other competition law, and, if so, to determine appropriate remedial action.

B.17 During 1998, OFTEL opened investigations into a wide range of competition issues, including BT's payphone access charge, BT's Friends and Family discounts scheme, and the pricing of National leased lines. OFTEL also conducted own initiative investigations into a number of BT's services and proposed tariffs. For example Corporate Advance, Dual and BT's Redcare Alarms. Some of the more notable cases concluded in 1998 are summarised below.

## WITHDRAWAL OF BT'S CAMPUS CONNECT

B.18  As reported in the 1997 annual report, the Director General concluded that BT was cross-subsidising its Campus Connect service at the end of December 1997. Campus Connect was an on-line administrative service providing mainly exam result notification to schools. Notice of the Director General's intention to issue a direction was sent to the interested parties during December 1997. The proposed direction would have required, among other remedial measures, recovery of Campus Connect's costs within six months.

B.19  In its response to the issue of the draft direction, BT announced that it was withdrawing Campus Connect, ceasing service in January 1999. BT also made representations saying that it would be impracticable for it to comply with the direction as it stood. OFTEL considered representations from both interested parties, and following further discussions BT agreed to withdraw Campus Connect in autumn 1998. Given BT's assurance that Campus Connect would not take on new customers up to its closure date, it was decided that there was no need for further regulatory action in respect of Campus Connect and this case was therefore closed.

B.20  However, at the time it announced that it was withdrawing Campus Connect, BT also announced the introduction of a new service, BT Connect to Business, to be launched in autumn 1998. According to BT, this service is targeted at business customers, but it appears that the service has some of the functionality of Campus Connect. However, the service has a very different price structure compared with Campus Connect. Following an allegation against BT Connect to Business that it has inherited the unfair subsidy that Campus Connect enjoyed, OFTEL is looking at BT Connect and its market to ensure that it is not being unfairly subsidised. OFTEL expects this exercise to be completed by the end of April 1999.

## BT'S COUNTRY CALLING PLANS

B.21  In April 1998, BT reported to OFTEL that it had sold a few hundred new Country Calling Plans for countries not then included in the plan over a short period in March 1998 without prior notification to OFTEL and/or without obtaining the necessary authorisation from OFTEL for the new schemes.

B.22  Following an investigation, OFTEL concluded that the sale of the plans without notification/authorisation did appear to constitute a breach of Condition 16(1)(b), in that BT departed from the terms and conditions of the Country Calling Plans scheme as published in BT's price list. However, as BT has taken a series of measures to remedy the breach and to avoid recurrence, the Director General is not satisfied the sale of the plans without notification/authorisation is likely to recur. Consequently, no enforcement action was taken. However, the Director General told BT that he may reconsider his position on this issue if any further breaches of Condition 16(1)(b) occur in the future.

B.23 For the same reason, the Director General is not satisfied that any breach of Conditions 17 and/or 24F resulting from the sale of unauthorised plans is likely to recur and therefore has not found it necessary to pursue the issue of whether Conditions 17 and/or 24F were breached in this case.

## BT'S FRIENDS AND FAMILY DISCOUNT SCHEME

B.24 In May, BT reported to OFTEL that it had given discounts on numbers nominated by a small percentage of its Friends and Family and BT Friends and Family Overseas outside the terms and conditions of those schemes.

B.25 Under the Friends and Family scheme, residential customers are entitled to receive a 10% discount on direct-dialled and self-dialled BT Chargecard calls to 11 nominated numbers. Customer may nominate one international and one mobile number. The eleventh number must be the customer's home number. Customer may also select one of the nominated numbers as BestFriend number that attracts a 20% discount.

B.26 Under BT Friends and Family Overseas, upon paying a quarterly subscription fee customers receive a 10% discount on direct-dialled and self-dialled BT Chargecard calls to five nominated international numbers.

B.27 Following an investigation, OFTEL concluded that, by giving additional discounts to some Friends and Family subscribers in contravention of the rules of the scheme, BT did appear to breach Condition 16(1)(b), in that it departed from the terms and conditions as published in BT's price list.

B.28 BT has told OFTEL that it has taken and/or intends to take a series of steps to remedy the breaches and to avoid a recurrence. These steps include a review of BT's billing systems, additional staff training and the generation of internal monthly reports listing any invalid calling circles, with managers being made responsible for making the necessary changes to correct any errors. Given these measures, the Director General is satisfied that discounts given in contravention of the rules of the Friends and Family schemes are unlikely to recur. For the same reasons, the Director General is not satisfied that any breach of Conditions 17 and/or 24F resulting from the additional discounts given unlikely to recur, and he has not therefore found it necessary to pursue the issue of whether Conditions 17 and/or 24F were breached.

B.29 Consequently no enforcement action was taken. However, OFTEL will continue to monitor whether BT implements the various steps it has said it will take to avoid recurrence.

## CWC'S (CABLE AND WIRELESS COMMUNICATIONS) 999 SERVICE

B.30 OFTEL received a complaint from Derbyshire Constabulary in late July 1998 stating that CWC's 999 operators had given incorrect customer addresses to emergency authorities on a number of occasions. This problem occurred on 'silent calls' where the calling party is unable to give an address to the operator or emergency authority and therefore their location has to be traced using CWC's computer database.

B.31 Following OFTEL enquiries, a manual solution was put in place on 13 August 1998 which resolved the problem in the short term. OFTEL has also received from CWC details of its plans to provide a permanent solution through a complete overhaul of the database used by 999 operators. This process has started and CWC provided OFTEL with weekly updates on progress. Once the database overhaul is complete, the entire system will be audited to ensure that the 999 service meets OFTEL's requirements. A final overhaul of the system was completed by March 1999.

B.32 CWC's actions satisfy OFTEL that initial steps have been taken and further measures are being put in place to ensure that emergency services are given correct addresses for customers. It is vital that the information provided to emergency authorities is correct, and OFTEL will continue to monitor the progress vigorously until it is fully satisfied that the permanent solution is complete and effective.

## BT'S CUSTOMER BILLING INFORMATION USED TO PROMOTE ITS NEW INTERNET SERVICE

B.33 On 11 September 1998, OFTEL received a complaint that some BT telesales staff were using Friends and Family Calling Circle information to identify customers who use the Internet. These customers were then being offered promotional material on BT Click, BT's first 'pay as you go' Internet service. OFTEL was concerned that BT was using information to which it alone has access and which is derived from a market (network access) in which it is dominant to promote a product in the Internet Service Provision market.

B.34 This appeared to OFTEL to be an abuse of BT's dominant position, in contravention of the Fair Trading Condition of its licence. This licence condition requires BT not to abuse its position of market dominance in an UK telecommunications market in a way that appreciably affects competition.

B.35 Following an investigation, on 23 September OFTEL concluded that BT's behaviour constituted a breach of Condition 18A.1 of the licence and BT stopped its marketing activity. Following this the Director General accepted an undertaking from BT that its telesales staff marketing BT Click Internet services will not have access to privileged customer calling information. BT has since provided details of how it has implemented this commitment to the satisfaction of the Director General.

B.36  The Director General has stated that if further incidents of this nature occur he will consider further action, which could include the issuing of an Order against BT.

## OFTEL CONCLUDES INVESTIGATION OF CALLS TO PERSONAL NUMBERING SERVICES

B.37  In early November 1998, OFTEL published conclusions of its investigation of a complaint made by Redstone Network Services Ltd (Redstone) about the cost of calling higher rate personal numbering (PN) services. Redstone complained that Vodafone was engaged in a discriminatory practice in that it had different (higher) prices for calls to the 07050 PN service (which might ultimately terminate on a Cellnet phone) compared with calls direct to an ordinary Cellnet number.

B.38  Redstone argued that there is no technical difference between the way Vodafone (in its function as a network that originates calls) handles calls to another operator's network (specifically Cellnet) which may then be diverted to another location and calls to Redstone's 07050 PN service.

B.39  Previously in March 1998, as part of its investigation, OFTEL published a consultative document *Personal Numbering Services* and sought views, particularly from personal numbering service providers and network operators. Responses were sought in relation to the competition issues arising from the Redstone complaint about the cost of calling higher rate personal numbering services. The consultative document also set out OFTEL's preliminary conclusions. OFTEL subsequently received complaints about Cellnet's personal numbering service, called 'Personal Assistant'. It was alleged that Cellnet was acting discriminately in its pricing of calls to Cellnet Personal Assistant relative to its pricing of calls to third party 'personal assistant' type personal numbering services. Calls to Personal Assistant were charged as calls to mobiles, while third party services attracted higher charges and were priced as calls to Special Services. During the investigation of these complaints, Cellnet increased its charges for calls to Redstone's 07050 service so that they were no longer charged at the same rate as calls to mobiles. This led OFTEL to look more widely at Cellnet's charges for calls to personal numbering services.

B.40  Following the consultation, and after taking all responses into account, the Director General concluded that there was a sufficient degree of demand-side substitutability between personal numbering services and mobile network embedded call divert services that the services should be regarded as being in the same product market.

B.41  In relation to the Redstone complaint about Vodafone, the Director General concluded that the higher prices that Vodafone was charging its subscribers for calls to Redstone were discriminatory and appeared to have a material detrimental impact on Redstone's business. Given that Vodafone's costs (its outpayments) were similar for calls to Redstone's 07050 service and for calls to Cellnet, OFTEL believed that Vodafone's retention rate should be similar for both types of calls.

B.42 Consequently, OFTEL concluded that Vodafone's pricing was unduly discriminatory within the meaning of Condition 9 of its licence. Vodafone was therefore advised that OFTEL expected that Vodafone's wholesale price to service providers for calls to 07050 (and similar personal numbering services) and for calls to Cellnet would differ by no more than the difference in outpayments.

B.43 Vodafone agreed to reduce its charges for calls to 07050 and other personal numbering services from 1 October 1998. These changes coincided with a separate, unrelated announcement from Vodafone that it had decided for commercial reasons to increase its prices for calls to non-Vodafone mobiles.

B.44 In relation to the complaints against Cellnet, OFTEL reached the view that for practical purposes its Personal Assistant service should be designated as a Full-Calling Party Pays personal numbering service – the calling party pays for the entire cost of the call (ie inbound plus the divert element). OFTEL therefore concluded that Cellnet should treat Personal Assistant and equivalent personal numbering services in the same way. In relation to the differential in prices for calling personal numbering services and mobiles, Cellnet was advised of the view OFTEL had reached following public consultation that services in the same market with similar outpayment costs should have similar retention levels and hence similar prices.

B.45 Cellnet was therefore asked for its proposals to remedy discrimination in its charging for calls to its Personal Assistant service, in relation both to calls to similar personal numbering services and to calls to mobile phones (which offer network embedded call divert services).

B.46 Cellnet agreed to make price changes that satisfy OFTEL's concerns about discriminatory pricing. Revised tariffs came into effect on 1 December 1998.

## PRICING OF NATIONAL LEASED LINES IN THE UK

B.47 In December 1997, OFTEL opened a preliminary investigation into the pricing of national leased lines in the UK following representations that prices were excessively high relative to those in the USA and in certain other European markets. OFTEL published a summary of this investigation *National Leased Lines in the UK* in early January 1999. The main conclusions and recommendations emerging are set out below.

◆ BT's cost information showed that overall returns for leased lines were positive, but below those made by the Retail Systems Business in total.

◆ International benchmarking studies were more favourable to BT's UK prices than the original representations. For an average basket of leased line lengths and for the majority of bandwidths, BT's UK prices were not significantly above those in the major European countries – about 10% above Germany and 10% below France. Short distance circuits in London are among the cheapest in the world.

◆ Competition in the provision of circuits of 2Mbit/s and above appears to be developing within the UK, and this has acted as a constraint on these prices in the absence of regulatory price controls.

◆ Competition for the provision of analogue circuits and digital circuits below 64kbit/s is limited. However, the price cap on these baskets acts as the constraint on prices and the incentive to improve efficiency. This price cap will be reviewed as part of the 2001 Price Control Review which will begin during 1999.

◆ Effective competition may be limited in certain areas because other operators will not always have sufficient infrastructure in place to offer customers a full end-to-end leased line service between any two locations and may therefore need to purchase 'final mile' circuits from other operators.

◆ Customers felt that this may impact on the quality of service they receive on such a line compared to that received on a leased line provided end-to-end over one network. There was little evidence that this was true, but it was recommended that Other Licence Operators (OLOs) address this perception.

◆ OFTEL was concerned that BT may be pricing these shorter distance 'final mile' circuits at relatively high levels in order to affect the competitiveness of other operators. The investigation found that BT does not appear to be pricing such circuits in a manner that distorts competition. However, it is recommended that, in order to facilitate the development of competition, where BT receives cost savings from providing such 'final mile' circuits to other operators, as opposed to other customers, these are reflected in the retail price charged.

B.48 OFTEL has invited comments on the conclusions and recommendations. During 1999 it will investigate the pricing of international leased lines.

## OFTEL'S ACTION ON UNSOLICITED FAXES

B.49 During 1998 OFTEL received nearly 4,000 complaints about the repeated sending of unsolicited faxes. OFTEL opened nine formal cases investigating whether companies sending unsolicited faxes had breached the conditions of the telecommunications licence under which they operate. Eight of these cases were opened to see whether the company complained about had committed a breach of Condition 6.1 of the Self Provision Licence (SPL) or Condition 7.1 of the Telecoms Services Licence (TSL). Under these conditions a licensee is prohibited from sending faxes for the purposes of advertising or the provision of goods to any person who requests that it cease sending such faxes.

B.50 In addition, an investigation was started to discover whether the British Fax Directory had breached Condition 6.2 of the TSL, which states that a licensee is prohibited from using automated calling equipment to search for fax numbers without obtaining the prior written consent of those called. The licensee must also maintain a record of those persons who consent to receive calls used to search for fax numbers.

B.51  OFTEL investigated complaints against the following companies in 1998:

- The British Fax Directory (BFD)/ Second Telecom/ Top 20 Ltd;

- 20th Century Fax;

- SNC Telecommunications;

- Crucial Input;

- Premium Competitions;

- Luckey Promotions;

- Tele-Check (First Report Ltd);

- Addwell Systems;

- Premium Phone Services Ltd.

B.52  In several of these cases, OFTEL received assurances from the company involved that it would comply with its licence obligations in the future. These assurances and the information OFTEL obtained gave the Director General satisfaction that no further action was necessary.

B.53  In the case involving BFD's use of automated calling equipment, the Director General issued a Final Order against BFD on 27 May 1998.

## BT'S FEATURENET

B.54  This case, one of the oldest handled by OFTEL, was brought to a successful conclusion in 1998. FeatureNet is BT's brand name for two types of service that offer customers a private, enhanced PBX-type service via the network. FeatureNet 1000 is a closed user group Virtual Private Network (VPN) which can include International FeatureNet; FeatureNet 5000 is a single site or multi site (Wide Area Centrex) service.

B.55  The case started as a complaint in 1995 that BT was unfairly cross subsidising its FeatureNet service given that BT's Number Retention package in BT's FeatureNet service was far cheaper than the Public Switched Telephone Network (PSTN) Call Divert service, yet was principally the same service. The investigation was subsequently widened to a review of the product offering as a whole. The main competition concerns were that:

- there was unfair cross subsidy of the FeatureNet service and BT was allowing FeatureNet to continue to operate unprofitably in a competitive market;

◆ PBX suppliers were being unfairly disadvantaged by the presence of a cross subsidy;

◆ FeatureNet customers were being offered preferential discounts on services that were not made available to other customers on comparable terms.

B.56 OFTEL examined BT's financial information to establish whether there was cross subsidy. As part of this examination, OFTEL consulted widely on the definition of the market in which FeatureNet operated. Based on the additional information received from industry through consultation, OFTEL concluded that the relevant market was the provision of VPN and Centrex services. Provision of PBXs was a separate market.

B.57 OFTEL's investigation concluded that:

◆ BT FeatureNet was making a loss and being cross-subsidised;

◆ market conditions have changed significantly since the complaint was made in 1995. In the case of the markets for Centrex and VPN's, BT's prices for new contracts were higher than those of its competitors and it was losing business to its competitors;

◆ there was insufficient evidence of undue preference or unduly discriminatory behaviour.

B.58 On the basis of the information available at the time, it was therefore unlikely that the cross subsidy was having a material effect on competition. There were strong indications that the market for VPN and Centrex services was becoming more competitive.

B.59 BT was asked to provide OFTEL with a compliance plan to move FeatureNet out of a position of cross subsidy, with specific milestones.

B.60 As a result of BT's move towards improved operating performance over the period, the competition case was closed. OFTEL will keep the market under review and take action if there is cause for further concern about effects on competition.

## BT REVISED ITS REDCARE ALARMS TARIFF

B.61 BT's RedCARE service monitors the integrity of telecommunications connections linking alarm monitoring stations operated by security companies with the premises of their customers. The system sends a frequent pulse up and down the connection acting like a radar. If the connection is broken, the alarm monitoring station is alerted immediately. In June 1997 OFTEL received a complaint about BT's charges for moving RedCARE connections between alarm monitoring stations.

B.62  According to the BT Price List, if all the connections at one alarm monitoring station were geographically transferred to another monitoring station owned by the same company, a flat fee of £5,000 was applicable. If, however, the central monitoring stations were not owned by the same company – for instance, if one company had acquired the connections of another – the transfer fee was £40 per connection. The complainant stated that prior to 1996 the £5,000 fee was applicable in both cases.

B.63  OFTEL discovered that the £40 per connection charge in fact applied to the reassignment of connections from one company to another. The payment of this charge enabled the acquiring company to pool the new connections with its existing connections and obtain a higher volume discount on all connections.

B.64  However, OFTEL still had concerns that the difference in charges applicable for the geographic transfer of connections depended on how the connections were acquired. For instance if an alarm monitoring company bought another outright – eg through share purchase – it could pay the £5,000 fee, whereas if only the connections were acquired it would have to pay £40 per connection. OFTEL asked BT to consider whether this differential charging may have represented undue discrimination, in contravention of BT's licence obligations.

B.65  BT denied that its charging represented a breach of its licence, but none-theless proposed changes to the charging structure. Subsequently, BT withdrew the £5,000 transfer fee and introduced a £2,000 charge for volume connection moves between monitoring stations regardless of their ownership. This charge was introduced in February 1998.

B.66  As this removed any possible discrimination between alarm monitoring companies, OFTEL closed this investigation.

## BT PROPOSED CORPORATE ADVANCE TARIFF

B.67  At the end of March and beginning of April BT consulted a number of its large business customers, OLOs and consumer organisations about a new tariff proposal called Corporate Advance. Comments on the scheme were to be sent to BT and OFTEL. The tariff was designed to offer business customers including other operators purchasing retail services from BT, an additional discount based on the totality of their core telecommunications expenditure aggregated across all sites in the UK. The extra discount would range from 1% to 4% for annual expenditure, starting at 1% for £5m pa, with the increments increasing by 0.5% for each £5m pa increase in expenditure. It was intended that the following core network services would count towards these discounts:

- All PSTN & ISDN call charges including Local, Regional, National & International;

◆ Calls to mobile, Premium Rate Services and Information Services;

◆ BT Chargecard call charges;

◆ Inbound Freefone 0800/0808 and Lo-call 0345/0845 call, connection and rental charges (where the customer purchases inbound services from BT);

◆ PSTN & ISDN line rental and connection charges;

◆ UK Private Circuits (analogue & digital) & Prime Service Circuit rentals & connections;

◆ International Private Leased Circuits rentals and connections;

◆ FeatureNet OffNet calls (excluding options a&b);

B.68 OFTEL followed up some of the responses from customers and Other Licensed Operators (OLOs) and had detailed discussions with BT on concerns raised by the proposed tariff. BT had notified OFTEL that it intended to introduce the tariff in July 1998 but as discussions had not been concluded, BT withdrew the tariff to allow time for further discussions. OFTEL will consult interested parties if BT come forward with a revised proposal.

## BT DUAL TARIFF

B.69 In December 1998 BT introduced its BT Dual discount scheme which offers business customers additional discounts on their UK call spend aggregated across all sites. The scheme offers discounts of between 1% and 5% for customers spending more than £125 per quarter on qualifying calls. The maximum discount of 5% is achieved at a quarterly spend of £1m. Calls included within the scheme are local and national calls, calls to mobile phones, FeatureNet OffNet calls and incoming Freefone and Lo-call calls.

B.70 The introduction of the BT Dual tariff followed an OFTEL statement published in October 1998 *Tariffing Issues: Bundling of Inbound and Outbound Services.* This statement set out OFTEL's assessment of the scheme and invited views on OFTEL's preliminary conclusion that the tariff's introduction would not appear to have a material adverse effect on competition. Responses to the statement did not lead OFTEL to alter this conclusion.

B.71 During 1998 BT also proposed tariff called Corporate Advance. This tariff caused concern as it bundled together a much broader range of products than the call services contained in BT Dual.

## ENFORCEMENT AND MONITORING

B.72 This section covers some of the cases, which resulted in formal enforcement action by the Director General under the Telecommunication Act 1984 or where he issued determinations to licensed operators under their licences during 1998.

B.73  During the year the Director General made a provisional order against Cellnet in relation to a new service provider payment plan. He also issued a final order against BT ordering it to publish an accurate and comprehensible price list. For the first time, the Director General made two orders to enforce the class licences – the Telcoms Services Licence and the Self Provision Licence. In August, the Director General determined the level of the payphone access charge by BT to users of freephone numbers for calls from BT's payphones. In December, the Director General made a determination on the review provision contained in BT's Standard Interconnect Agreement under Network Charge Controls.

B.74  The legal effect of an order made under Section 16 of the Telecommunications Act 1984 is that it gives third parties who suffer loss from any future breach of the order the right to bring an action for damages or injunction against the company which is the subject of the order. If the order is breached, the Director General can also seek a court order to enforce it, breach of which later would be contempt of court.

B.75  Some of the more notable investigations, which resulted in enforcement action, are summarised below.

## CELLNET ORDERED TO STOP UNFAIR PRICING

B.76  On 1 November 1997, Cellnet introduced a new Payment Plan setting out the wholesale payment terms on which it would provide airtime to service providers. In response to complaints from independent service providers, OFTEL opened an investigation into the terms of the plan. OFTEL found that bonuses and discounts available to service providers under the plan were constructed in such a way that they skewed benefits towards larger service providers, threatening the ability of smaller independent service providers to compete on a fair basis. In practice, those standing to benefit most from the new plan's payment structure were tied service providers with ownership links to Cellnet. It appeared to the Director General that the payment terms offered amounted to undue discrimination against independent service providers in breach of the terms of Cellnet's licence.

B.77  On 12 February, he made a provisional order requiring Cellnet to bring the discrimination to a halt, and to produce a compliance plan.

B.78  Cellnet made some modifications to the plan in response to concerns raised in the run up to the provisional order. Following the order, Cellnet embarked on a wider review of its financial arrangements with service providers, consulting them in the process. While welcoming this move, the Director General gave notice in March of his intention to make a final order unless the review resulted in an outcome fully consistent with Cellnet's licence.

B.79  On 28 April, Cellnet presented OFTEL with its proposals for a completely revised payment plan starting on 1 July, following its consultation with service providers. Having considered representations received from service providers and others in response to the statutory notice, and taking account of Cellnet's appointment of a compliance officer, the Director General announced on 11 May that that there was no need for further enforcement action against Cellnet in respect of the payment plan.

### BT ORDERED TO IMPROVE PUBLICATION OF ITS PRICE LIST

B.80 In February 1998, the DG issued a final order finding BT in breach of Condition 16 of licence and requiring BT to publish an accurate and comprehensible price list in accordance with that condition. Condition 16 broadly speaking requires BT to publish a list of its prices and to ensure it does not depart from those published prices.

B.81 The order followed an own-initiative investigation, which was conducted after OFTEL discovered a number of tariffs were missing from BT's Price List. Despite OFTEL having prompted BT to review its systems to ensure that the Price List was accurate and clear, OFTEL subsequently found further examples of unclear or ambiguous entries.

B.82 OFTEL considers that it is vital that BT's Price List is accurate and comprehensible so that BT's customers and competitors know the products BT offers, how they are charged and their terms and conditions. The Director also needs to be able to rely on the Price List so as to ensure that BT offers the same tariffs to customers in the same or comparable position.

B.83 To ensure BT adheres to its obligations under Condition 16 of its licence and the terms of the order, it has devised Project Seachange to review its current pricing processes, its Price List and its billing systems. The Seachange Programme has been divided into 14 work packages and is designed to encourage pro-active monitoring of its pricing processes. Some of the issues the work packages are designed to address include the clarity and accuracy of the Price List and the development of a compensation scheme for competitors who incur damages because of errors in the Price List.

B.84 In Autumn 1998, OFTEL met with BT to discuss the work packages of the Seachange project, in particular to ensure they adequately addressed OFTEL's concerns about BT's Price List. BT submits progress reports on the work packages to OFTEL on a quarterly basis and meets informally with OFTEL to discuss any outstanding issues.

### THE BRITISH FAX DIRECTORY ORDERED TO STOP FAXFINDING USING AUTOMATED CALLING EQUIPMENT

B.85 In July last year, OFTEL received a complaint from an organisation stating that it had been subjected to unsolicited fax finding calls from the British Fax Directory

(BFD) using automated calling equipment. The BFD is a provider of telecommunications services under the Class Licence to Run Branch Systems to Provide Telecommunications Services (the TSL) granted by the Secretary of State under Section 7 of the Telecommunications Act 1984.

B.86 In the course of OFTEL's investigation BFD admitted that it did have an automated system which rings numbers for the purpose of establishing whether or not there is a fax on the other end. Condition 6 of the TSL prohibits the use of automated calling equipment for this purpose without the prior consent of the recipient of the call and requires the licensee to keep a record of persons who have so consented. Again BFD admitted that it had no records of persons who had given their prior consent to this.

B.87 On 31 March 1998 the Director General issued a notice that he proposed to make a final order against BFD on the basis that BFD was in breach of Condition 6.2(a) of the TSL and it was likely to breach it again. BFD made representations in respect of the notice that BFD had stopped all faxfinding and that therefore there was no likelihood that they would breach again. The Director General took this into consideration in deciding whether to make a final order.

B.88 However, the Director General was not assured by the licensee's statement, particularly considering that the licensee was a company engaged in the business of sending out faxes, and for that reason had an obvious commercial desire to know as many fax numbers as possible throughout the UK. The Director also considered that contravention of condition 6.2 (a) was capable of causing disruption and distress to those persons on the receiving end of the calls. Such a practice also prevents the recipient of the calls from making or receiving other calls whilst their line is subject to fax finding calls.

B.89 The final order was made on 27 May 1998 requiring BFD to cease using automated dialling equipment to search for fax numbers without prior consent from the call recipients. It was also ordered to maintain a record of those who have consented to receiving calls for the purpose of searching fax numbers.

## JAMES E JAMES LTD ORDERED TO STOP MAKING UNSOLICITED TELESALES CALLS

B.90 On 30 July 1998 the Director General issued a Final Order under Section 16 of the Telecommunications Act 1984 against James E James Ltd for repeatedly making sales calls after being asked to stop.

B.91 James E James are an advertising contractors and printers who OFTEL had requested to stop calling the Greek Taverna in Carshalton Surrey attempting to sell advertising space. The proprietor of the Greek Taverna had made complaints about this company dating back to May 1996. James E James admitted making calls after promising not to. They also said that they could not provide an absolute guarantee that they would not call people who did not want to be called.

B.92  James E James operate their telephones under the terms of the Self Provision Licence. Condition 6.1 (a) of this licence states that if a person requests that the licensee should stop making advertising or sales calls to them they must abide by those wishes. James E James' repeated calls to the Greek Taverna have placed them in breach of their licence.

B.93  On 17 June 1998 the Director General issued a notice under Section 17 of the Telecommunications Act 1984 that he proposed to issue a Final Order. Interested parties were invited to make representations to him on this matter. Several representations were made. After these were all considered carefully, the Director General decided to proceed with a Final Order banning James E James from making sales calls to persons who have requested that they cease doing so.

### DETERMINATION OF THE PAYPHONE ACCESS CHARGE

B.94  The Payphone Access Charge (PAC) is a charge made by BT to users of freephone numbers (e.g. starting with 0800, 0500) for calls from payphones. The PAC is levied because BT does not receive any revenue for freephone calls from payphones, although it bears the costs of providing a payphone network. A significant group of users of 0800 and 0500 numbers are indirect access operators offering calling card services mainly used for international calls. BT increased the level of the PAC on 1 December 1997 from 6.87 pence per minute (ppm) to 8.61 ppm. A number of operators complained about this increase. BT has to levy the PAC to itself as an internal transfer charge to all its payphone calls including Chargecard calls to ensure fair competition.

B.95  After a detailed examination of BT's costs and in-depth discussion with interested parties the Director General determined in August 1998 that the service of providing access to indirect access operator services is not competitive because of the combination of BT's dominance of payphone ownership in the UK, the UK-wide geographic scope of BT's payphone network and the small likelihood of other firms developing competing networks even if the PAC is set at an excessive level. The Director General also determined that the PAC should be 8.1 ppm backdated to 1 December 1997.

B.96  OFTEL will review the appropriate basis for the future regulation of the PAC with effect from October 1998. OFTEL has proposed that the charge should be subject to indexation by an RPI-X factor in order to avoid the need for annual regulatory review of the PAC.

### DETERMINATION OF REVIEW PROVISION OF BT'S INTERCONNECT AGREEMENTS

B.97  Following implementation of Network Charge Control (NCC) on 1 October 1997, BT updated its Standard Interconnect Agreement to reflect the new arrangements. As part of the new terms in the Agreement, BT sought to introduce a revised procedure whereby they could propose changes to the charges they pay other operators for interconnect services. BT offered the revised NCC Inter-connect Agreement to all operators.

B.98  The majority of operators signed the NCC Interconnect Agreement, accepting the new procedures including that related to their own services. However, One 2 One ( MPCL) disputed the procedure which would allow BT, at any time, to propose revised charges payable to MPCL's for interconnection services. MPCL were concerned that BT's ability to offer revised interconnect charges other than by a regular annual review process had the potential to undermine its revenue forecasts creating instability. MPCL asked the Director General to determine the terms in the Agreement.

B.99  In December 1998, having taken into consideration the views of the parties involved, the Director General determined that BT's proposed procedures for BT to propose changes to One 2 One's charges at any time were reasonable and should appear in the revised contract. In taking this view, the Director General noted that:

◆ all other operators including other mobile operators had accepted the revised Standard Contract and it was undesirable for One 2 One's terms to be different;

◆ any proposal by BT for a change to One 2 One's charges would not apply unless One 2 One agreed and in the event of a dispute over a particular proposal, that the matter could be referred to the Director General for determination;

◆ Annual reviews as favoured by MPCL would prevent BT from being able to respond to market changes.

## COMPETITION ACT 1998

B.100  The Competition Bill completed its passage through both Houses of Parliament during the year and received Royal Assent on 9 November 1998. Throughout 1998 OFTEL was involved in discussions with the industry, the Office of Fair Trading and other Government departments over the development of the Bill. In particular, OFTEL played a key role in the Concurrency Working Group, comprised of the regulators and OFT, working on practical implementation issues such as the development of guidelines on how the new Act will be applied.

B.101  The Government intends that the new prohibitions contained in the Act on the abuse of a dominant position and the making of anti-competitive agreements will come into force in March 2000. Under the Act the Director General may, for example:

◆ give guidance on the application of the Act;

♦ consider complaints about breach of the prohibitions;

♦ impose interim measures to prevent serious and irreparable damage;

♦ give decisions on the application of the Act to specific agreements or conduct;

♦ carry out investigations in response to complaints or on his own initiative;

♦ impose financial penalties;

♦ give and enforce directions to bring an infringement to an end;

♦ issue general advice and information on how the Act applies in his sector.

B.102   In the interim period before the prohibitions come into force, OFTEL may give early guidance to companies as to whether a particular agreement entered into since Royal Assent would contravene the 'Chapter I' prohibition dealing with agreements were it in force. OFTEL had not received any request for early guidance by the end of the year.

B.103   One of the important issues dealt with by the Concurrency Working Group were the guidelines on *Concurrent application to regulated industries*. These were published in draft in November 1998 for public consultation. They explained which industry sectors were subject to concurrent jurisdiction by the Director General of Fair Trading and a sector regulator. It also explained the procedures involved and gave information on how the regulators work together. For example, it was agreed that formal notification of agreements and conduct for guidance or a decision should be sent to the Office of Fair Trading (OFT) but where the agreement or conduct notified fell within the jurisdiction of a regulator, he would normally deal with the case.

B.104   In preparation for the Act, OFTEL begun work on guidelines on the application of the new Act within the telecommunications sector. More practical issues such as the training of casework officers and OFTEL's internal casework procedures were also addressed. OFTEL expects to continue to work closely with OFT and the other regulators throughout 1999 on these issues.

## GUIDELINES ON COMPETITION ACT

B.105   The purpose of OFTEL's guidelines is to provide information not only on OFTEL's procedures but also on how specific competition issues will be dealt with.

B.106   The Competition Act 1998 is enforced concurrently by the Director General of the Fair Trading and the sector regulators. In conjunction with the regulators, the Director General of Fair Trading is required to prepare and publish advice and information, in the form of guidelines, on the application and enforcement of the prohibitions. The regulators can also issue guidelines specific to the sectors in which they have concurrent jurisdiction with the Director General of Fair Trading.

B.107   OFTEL, in conjunction with the Office of Fair Trading, issued *Guidelines on the application of the Competition Act in the telecommunications sector* for consultation in January 1999.

B.108   The guidelines are intended to set out the general principles that the Director General of Telecommunications and the Director General of Fair Trading expect to apply when exercising powers under the Competition Act in the tele-communications sector.

B.109   As the telecommunications sector in most European Union Member States has only been recently opened up to competition, there is limited jurisprudence in the application of Articles 85 and 86 of the EC Treaty to the sector. This, combined with the technological, economic and historical factors that make the sector different, necessitates telecommunications sector specific guidelines. The guidelines will enable those who are involved in the telecommunications sector, and those who consider themselves to have been affected by anti-competitive behaviour, to assess better for themselves the circumstances in which particular types of behaviour are likely to be prohibited.

## SCOPE OF THESE GUIDELINES

B.110   The guidelines, which will be consistent with the Competition Act guidelines produced by the OFT and the regulators, set out the approach that will be taken in applying and enforcing the Competition Act in the telecommunications sector. They will focus on market definition, the assessment of market power and the assessment of individual agreements and conduct in the telecommunications sector. The guidelines will concentrate on areas where the idiosyncrasies of the telecommunications sector mean that a different emphasis or a slightly different approach in the application of the Competition Act is likely in the telecommuni-cations sector while at the same time ensuring consistency with the guidelines produced by the OFT and the regulators.

B.111   There will be a consultation on the guidelines and a workshop in February 1999 to discuss the guidelines with industry and consumer bodies.

## Regulatory Framework for service providers

### FIXED NETWORKS

B.112   Following lengthy discussion with OFTEL, BT launched Calls and Access, its first major service provider product. Currently available only as a single-line product, Calls and Access allows service providers (and other licensed operators) to take contractual responsibility for a BT line and then resell the use of that line to the end user. BT continues to maintain the line and provides the service provider with bulk billing data; however, all contact with the customer is channelled through the service provider, who may choose to combine the service with other features such as Indirect Access to alternative networks. OFTEL agreed in 1997 that, if BT wishes to provide such services to service providers at prices that may be preferential to those offered to the generality of end users, this will not be viewed as a breach of BT's licence obligations concerning undue preference. OFTEL believes that products such as Calls and Access will allow service providers to offer customers a wider choice of competitive services.

## MOBILE NETWORKS

B.113  Regulatory obligations on mobile operators to supply wholesale airtime to independent service providers came under close scrutiny in 1998. The primary purpose of these obligations is to ensure that customers have the widest possible choice of services and service providers. OFTEL believes that, in a fully competitive market, the reasonable needs of independent service providers for wholesale airtime will be met without regulatory controls. However, where competition is less vigorous, regulatory intervention may be necessary.

B.114  On 2 April 1998, following a number of consultations, including a statutory public consultation, OFTEL made changes to the licences of Orange and One 2 One which had the effect of removing from those licences the obligation to provide wholesale airtime to mobile service providers. The decision was taken on the basis that these two operators did not have market power and would be better placed to develop their businesses in competition with Cellnet and Vodafone, who did have market power, if they were allowed to distribute their products in the manner which they considered to be in their best interests. It was this decision to modify Orange and One 2 One's licences that was the subject of judicial review.

B.115  The challenge from a number of service providers was based on the grounds that the Director General had failed to have regard to his duties and functions under the Telecommunications Act in removing the obligation from the Orange and One 2 One licences. Two other issues were included in the application for judicial review: an application requiring the Director General to enforce the cross subsidy condition and a claim that the definition of a Well Established Operator (WEO) unlawfully allowed the Director General to impose obligations on operators in circumstances where there was a lack of transparency.

B.116  At a hearing in the High Court in November 1998 Mr Justice Lightman dismissed the application for judicial review. He decided that the Director General had a duty to ensure that all reasonable demands for telecommunications services were met, but it was for him as the expert to decide how those demands should be met. The Director General had to balance the competing and sometimes conflicting duties in Section 3 of the Telecommunications Act and it was not for the Court to revisit the decision unless there was a material error in the decision making process or the Director acted irrationally. The judge also said that the Director General's published policy that he would not normally regard cross subsidy as unfair where an operator did not have market power was acceptable and within his statutory powers. Also the circumstances when an operator would be deemed to be Well Established did not have to appear on the face of the licence provided the definition was clear as the judge decided it was.

B.117 This is the first time that the duties of the Director General have been examined by the courts in this detail and the judgement provides a very helpful guide to how the Director General should interpret his duties and responsibilities under the Telecommunications Act.

B.118 Over the same period, OFTEL started an internal review of whether the other two operators, Vodafone and Cellnet, still had market power and should continue to be obliged to supply independent service providers with wholesale airtime on a non discriminatory basis. That review also included a re-appraisal of the terms on which Vodafone and Cellnet were supplying wholesale airtime.

## SERVICE PROVIDER ACCESS TO FIXED AND MOBILE NETWORKS

B.119 In December 1998, as part of an exercise to ensure that UK licences comply with the requirements of the EC Licensing Directive, the DTI published proposals for modifying the licences of all fixed and mobile operators. The draft licences include revised text dealing with the requirements on fixed and mobile operators to provide access to the networks at points other than those offered to the majority of end users. These requirements, commonly known as 'Special Network Access', are expected to facilitate service provider access to networks; a necessary condition for the development of many more complex innovative services for customers. In 1999, OFTEL will publish guidelines on the implementation of these provisions.

## OFTEL CONTACT WITH SERVICE PROVIDERS

B.120 During 1998, management of OFTEL's work with service providers was brought within the Network and Services Competition Directorate and, subsequently within the newly formed Policy Directorate. This has made it easier to address the inevitable tension between the promotion of both infrastructure investment and services competition. The Service Provider Forum, hosted by OFTEL every other month, has been further developed as a platform for addressing service provider issues and a wide range of OFTEL staff have spoken at these meetings. OFTEL's programme of outreach visits to service provider companies has continued to provide OFTEL with valuable insights into the pressures and obstacles faced by service providers.

# C. **Services for the Information Age**

## Access to bandwidth

C.1 A key feature of the changing telecommunications market is the high importance of data services. The provision of 'higher bandwidth' services such as high-speed Internet access and video-on-demand will become increasingly important in both the fixed and mobile sectors. Bandwidth refers to the speed at which information can be transferred; more bandwidth is needed to deliver advanced services.

C.2 In December 1998, OFTEL issued an important consultation document, *Access to Bandwidth – Bringing Higher Bandwidth Services to the Consumer.* This examines current and future demand for advanced services; how these might best be delivered to consumers; and whether – and if so how – OFTEL might need to intervene to promote their delivery, using higher-bandwidth technology. The consultation aims to generate active debate rather than to present firm proposals. Added impetus for the consultation is provided both by technological advances and by the increasing EU-level discussion, in which OFTEL is participating actively, of 'local loop unbundling' (see below).

C.3 OFTEL's preliminary view is that advanced services can best be supplied widely and early using BT's own direct lines ('copper loops') to customers. BT's lines serve about 85% of homes in the UK, so they are well placed to deliver advanced services to residential customers, as well as to those small and medium-sized business users who cannot afford the leased lines already used by large companies to access advanced services. Higher-bandwidth equipment, probably using 'Digital Subscriber Line (DSL)' technology, would have to be added to BT's copper loops as part of the process of delivering advanced services over BT's network. While there are alternatives to using BT's local loops – cable networks, satellite and radio – none of these is as yet widely commercially exploited.

C.4 The consultation document considered whether BT's copper loops should be 'unbundled' and made available for other companies to provide the services to customers. This was one of five options presented for providing advanced services over BT's copper loops. One other option is a full higher-bandwidth public network, which could make possible calls to many suppliers, as available now for basic telephony.

C.5 Issues to consider include the price that competitors would pay to BT under each option (which could affect investment by BT and others in new and better networks); managing the potential interference between different higher-bandwidth lines; and the effects on customers' choice of operator (both for higher-bandwidth and basic telephony services).

## Electronic commerce

C.6 The Department of Trade and Industry (DTI) will introduce an Electronic Commerce Bill in 1999 to establish a voluntary licensing framework for trust service providers. On 19 October 1998, the DTI announced their intention that OFTEL will be the initial licensing authority. Trust service providers are the organisations that issue encryption key pairs – whether for the purpose of providing a service such as a confidentiality service (to protect electronic data against unauthorised disclosure) or an electronic signature service (to authenticate individuals or organisations). Such services are of great importance to the future development of electronic commerce. OFTEL expects to work closely with DTI and members of the industry over the coming months to develop the proposed framework for these services.

## Internet policy

C.7 OFTEL has established a separate project focusing on Internet policy with the objective of identifying emerging issues arising from developments in the Internet industry. It is not the intention to develop a separate regulatory framework – the Internet is already subject to telecommunications regulation and other legislation elsewhere. In this, OFTEL's interest will focus on issues of access to and carriage across IP networks – not the value-added 'content' services provided over the Internet which are highly competitive. Among other issues, OFTEL will be looking at the cost of accessing the Internet. The principal concern is to ensure that regulatory barriers do not emerge to the continuing development of the Internet and the services provided over it.

## Internet access for schools

C.8 OFTEL continued its work to ensure that schools have access to the information superhighway. Following OFTEL's consultation document *Access to the Superhighways for Schools,* published in October 1997, BT introduced two new service packages to connect schools to the Internet in April 1998. Other telecommunication companies have also responded to the need for predictable and low tariffs by offering a variety of special deals for schools.

C.9 BT's Schools Internet Caller offers the option of two different service packages, both of which are available at a considerable discount from the normal tariff. Schools can choose either a 'dial-up' service using the Public Switched Telephone Network or a digital service using the Integrated Services Digital Network (which allows faster access to on-line services). These services allow unlimited access to the Internet via any independent service provider or on-line services provider between 8.00 am and 6.00 pm, Mondays to Fridays during term time. In Hull, Kingston Communications also provides special tariff packages for local schools. A number of independent service providers offer special tariff packages to schools in conjunction with other telecommunications operators.

C.10 All the cable companies use their local loops to provide Internet access to schools within their franchises. Each offers various packages with special tariffs for on-line access for schools and colleges. There is a range of options, including dial-up and ISDN access. Some also offer discounts on broadband access. Operators use either their own Internet gateway or an independent service provider.

C.11 Most schools now have a choice of supplier, offering a range of fixed and affordable prices for Internet access. OFTEL continues to work with the industry to explore the possibilities of reductions in price for primary schools and special tariffs for broadband access.

## Convergence and communications in the future

C.12 The telecommunications market, particularly the systems over which services are delivered, is undergoing a period of rapid change. The advances in digital and compression technologies are breaking down the old distinctions between networks and industries. Data traffic is outstripping voice traffic on most networks. Wireless telephony is challenging the pre-eminence of fixed line operators. Increasingly, the communications market is changing to become globally focused and data-based with players and alliances within and across the traditional boundaries of telecommunications, broadcasting and IT. OFTEL has a central role in the development of the knowledge-driven economy. Telecommunications networks will form the backbone for the delivery of new services. OFTEL's role will remain the same, to obtain the best deal for the consumer, but the way in which we regulate will need to change as the market does.

C.13 These changes have prompted both the European Commission and the UK Government to review the regulatory frameworks governing the communications sector. OFTEL welcomes and supports these initiatives. Fast-moving markets and different speeds in the development of competition between different service markets make an overly prescriptive approach to regulation inappropriate. Such an approach will lead to over-regulation, which in turn can lead to underinvestment and lack of innovation and/or to under-regulation, and lack of real competition, in areas where the dominant player retains control.

### UK

C.14 In March, Don Cruickshank, the then Director General, was asked to give evidence to the House of Commons Select Committee on Culture Media and Sport as part of the Committee's Inquiry into audio-visual communications and the regulation of broadcasting. Prior to his appearance, OFTEL submitted two submissions to the Inquiry outlining its views on the future regulation of the communications sector. The Committee produced a report, *The Multi-Media Revolution* setting out its recommendations.

C.15 In July, the Government published a consultation document, *Regulating Communications:Approaching Convergence in the Information Age,* setting out the Government's preliminary views on the likely implications of digital convergence for the legal and regulatory frameworks covering broadcasting and telecommunications. It sought to test those views by asking a series of questions. OFTEL submitted a response, which developed some of the key themes set out the two earlier submissions to the Inquiry.

## EU

C.16 In December 1997, the European Commission produced a Green Paper, *On the Convergence of the Telecommunications, Media and Information Technology Sectors, and the Implications for Regulation,* to which OFTEL responded. In August, the EU published a follow-up paper summarising the responses and asking three additional questions. It was made clear that the majority of the issues raised in the original Green Paper would be taken forward within the context of the 1999 Review of telecommunications legislation. (For further details about the 1999 Review refer to section G of this report on European and International Activities).

C.17 OFTEL's responses had a common theme. The key points were:

◆ given the strong evidence on convergence between networks, there is a need to ensure coherent and consistent economic regulation across the converging sectors in order to promote regulatory certainty and investment;

◆ the need to create the appropriate balance between regulation based on a competition law approach and more traditional regulation to deal with market failures and the delivery of social goals, while ensuring the protection of consumers;

◆ that any sector-specific rules used should be based on a clear rationale and objectives; be justified rigorously against the agreed objectives; and be flexible enough to deal with new problems as they arise. Such rules should form a coherent whole with existing horizontal competition and consumer protection law. There must also be a quick way of removing rules designed for problems that no longer exist;

◆ the importance of access, which spans the spectrum from, at one end, access to networks by service providers and competing operators, through access to technical information to, at the other end, access by consumers to information and services. Addressing these issues requires a delicate balance between promoting the interests of consumers and ensuring that the resulting burdens placed on industry are not so great as to discourage investment and adversely impact on the quality, diversity and price of communications services available to the consumer.

C.18  In the light of these changes, OFTEL must be flexible and proactive. As part of developing the Management Plan for 1999/2000, OFTEL will review both its short- and its long-term strategy so that it can have a coherent and consistent approach. Pending future legislation, OFTEL will seek to develop existing co-operative arrangements between regulators. OFTEL will work with them to develop, as far as is possible within the existing legislation, a coherent approach to economic regulation across the converging sectors.

## Digital television

C.19  Mass-market digital television arrived in the UK in autumn 1998 with the launch of the digital satellite service promoted by BSkyB. A number of other broadcasters opted to transmit their services via this platform. Digital terrestrial transmission featuring existing free-to-air and new (mostly free-to-air) channels from the BBC and the Channel 3, 4, and 5 companies plus a range of pay channels from *On Digital* followed later in the year. Digital cable launches are expected during 1999.

C.20  Overall, this will generate an explosion in viewer choice. In addition to a vast increase in the number of channels available, viewers will (from mid-1999) be able to use their television as a gateway to interactive services such as home shopping and banking and to on-line information services and games.

C.21  In 1995, the Government decided that OFTEL should have the responsibility for regulating conditional access systems for digital broadcasting, in particular the requirements of the EU Advanced Television Standards Directive. The phrase 'conditional access' is used to describe the systems and technology by which access to television programmes is restricted to those viewers that have paid for them. OFTEL worked closely with the DTI to create the Advanced Television Standards Regulations (SI 1996 No 3151) and the Conditional Access Class Licence, which was issued on 7 January 1997.

C.22  The thrust of the regulatory regime is to ensure that content providers can obtain conditional access services on fair, reasonable and non-discriminatory terms; and in particular that control of conditional access technology is not used to distort, restrict or prevent competition in television and other content services. It also seeks to maximise consumer choice by allowing viewers, as far as possible, to access services on more than one delivery mechanism and have easy access to comprehensive information about the range of services available and ease of selection of those services.

C.23  Key provisions in the Conditional Access Class Licence include a requirement for licensees to offer technical conditional access services on fair, reasonable and non-discriminatory terms and to cooperate with cable operators to ensure cost-effective transcontrol (a means of translating or replacing one type of conditional access service with another).

C.24 The Government subsequently decided that a broadly equivalent regime should apply in respect of control over end user access to digital interactive and information services, whether delivered by broadcasting networks or otherwise. This 'access control' regime was incorporated into various Class Licences with effect from the beginning of 1998.

C.25 Throughout the year, OFTEL liaised closely with market players, consumer representatives and other regulators with a view to ensuring that there would be no legitimate concerns about anti-competitive practices that might delay the launch of digital television and, subsequently, digital interactive and on-line information services via TV. This state of preparedness was one of the factors taken into account by the European Commission (DGIV) in its consideration of clearance under European competition law of the British Interactive Broadcasting (BIB) joint venture.

## Liaison with other regulators

C.26 OFTEL deepened its working relationship with the Independent Television Commission (ITC) and the Office of Fair Trading over broadcasting issues during 1998. The aim is to improve the coherence of the UK regulatory regime as a whole. An informal 'Group of 3' mechanism has been set up to keep one another abreast of progress on issues of common interest; and to take forward certain issues in partnership. An example of the latter is a joint ITC/OFTEL consultation planned for Spring 1999 on the bundling of TV and telephony, building on some earlier work by the ITC. The same parties also hold regular collective discussions on regulatory policy issues with DCMS and the Competition Policy and Communications and Information Industries Directorates of DTI via the 'Group of 6' forum.

# D. **Numbering Issues**

D.1   Number portability, national code and number change issues and an OFTEL proposal to charge operators for the use of numbers to promote their efficient use were the main focus of OFTEL's Numbering Unit during the year.

## National code and number change

D.2   OFTEL continued to work throughout the year with industry, via various steering and working groups, to minimise the inconvenience to customers of the national code and number changes necessary to implement the National Numbering Scheme. This scheme, which was announced by OFTEL in January 1997, is intended to provide customers with a clear indication of the type of service they are calling, simply by looking at the initial digits of a telephone number. The scheme is also designed to be sufficiently robust to meet future demands for numbers and to be flexible enough to adapt to new technologies and services.

D.3   The scheme allocates two-digit prefixes to different types of service.

| | |
|----|----|
| 00 | International |
| 01 | Existing area codes |
| 02 | New area codes – beginning in 1999 |
| 03 | Reserved for more area codes |
| 04 | Spare |
| 05 | Reserved for corporate use |
| 06 | Spare |
| 07 | Personal, paging and mobile numbers |
| 08 | Special services (Freephone, local rate, national rate) |
| 09 | Premium rate services |

D.4   The industry campaign to communicate the changes, backed by OFTEL, began early in 1998. However, the first significant wave of publicity appeared in the summer with a series of adverts using the slogan 'The Big Number'. During the rest of the year the primary focus was on getting the code and number change message through to businesses, which will need to ensure that their phone systems and databases are modified as well as to make arrangements for stationery and signage etc.

## Number portability

D.5   Following modifications to the mobile operators' licences in 1997, requiring the introduction of mobile number portability, OFTEL spent 1998 carefully monitoring the industry's progress toward implementation. Although the target date was fairly challenging, mobile network operators and mobile airtime service providers developed processes to support portability and successfully tested both the technical and administrative systems in the autumn and winter. The implementation of mobile portability was launched in January 1999.

D.6    Customer demand to port their geographic telephone numbers continued to rise. By the end of 1998, the number of operators with portability had increased and the total of ported numbers exceeded half a million. In addition, multi-line enhancements to geographic portability were launched for Basic-rate ISDN portability (excluding European ISDN which is expected in 1999) and Direct Dial In (DDI) number ranges.

D.7    In March, OFTEL determined the charges BT can make for the provision of non-geographic number portability to other operators. Portability of Premium Rate Service numbers was rolled out during the summer.

D.8    In November, OFTEL held the first meeting of an industry focus group assembled to devise an appropriate method of introducing number portability for personal numbers by January 2000.

## European number portability developments

D.9    The current number portability regime in the UK, whereby telephone subscribers can retain their telephone numbers when they change operators, works on the principle of reciprocal agreement between 'consenting' operators. Two new European Union Directives were adopted in 1998 that will affect this regime: the Revised Voice Telephony Directive (98/10/EC) and the Numbering Directive (98/61/EC). The Numbering Directive will change the existing portability arrangements. At present, portability depends upon a decision by operators as to whether they wish to offer it. (BT is the only operator that must enter into reciprocal portability agreements with other operators if requested to do so.) In future, portability will be driven by the customer – portability by subscriber request.

D.10 OFTEL has been working with industry representatives on how best to implement the Numbering Directive's provisions, which will become effective on 1 January 2000. The Directive covers portability for both geographic numbers (numbers relating to fixed geographic locations) and non-geographic numbers. For example, personal and premium rate numbers.

## New arrangements for numbering administration

D.11 OFTEL published a consultative document in July proposing changes to the management of the UK's Numbering Scheme. The document looked at ways in which charging operators for numbers could promote greater efficiency and increased stability in the numbering scheme. The consultation also set out proposals for allocating freephone, local and other specially tariffed numbers directly to customers from a central independent body.

D.12 OFTEL currently allocates blocks of numbers to operators free of charge. With no value placed on the numbering resource, there is little incentive for operators to be efficient in using numbers, and number hoarding may take place. This precipitates number shortages and increases the likelihood of number changes. The consultative document considered a possible future regime of charging for number blocks encompassing both auctions and administrative pricing.

D.13 For non-geographic ranges such as freephone and premium rate, OFTEL proposed to move away from the allocation of numbers in blocks and to introduce allocations of individual numbers directly to end users. This would give customers increased choice and more rights in numbers. The document proposed that partnerships with private sector bodies – Number Allocation Organisations (NAOs) – should be developed to carry out the new administrative functions, including the auctioning of numbers to end users. An option was also put forward for the contracting out to an NAO of the administration function currently carried out by OFTEL, the allocation of blocks to operators.

D.14 The consultation ran until December. The implementation of policy emerging from the consultation would be dependent on the availability of a suitable legislative vehicle.

## Freephones

D.15 In July 1998 a consultation document, *Freephone Numbers: Options for the Future,* was published. This identified seven options for the future of freephone numbers. Comments were sought on these options and responders were also invited to present other feasible options. The initial consultation period, which ran until 16 October 1998, was extended to 13 November 1998. A significant number of responses to the consultation were from users who requested that there should be no change to their existing 0800 9-digit number, because of the considerable costs involved in such a change, and that a way should be found to allow them to keep their numbers. Costs in the region of £500 million were suggested. Consequently, OFTEL is currently considering the technical feasibility of alternative options for generating more 0800 numbers without changing existing numbers, and will also carry out its own study into the costs of any changes. Following these pieces of work, OFTEL will hold a workshop in 1999 to consider the results and develop the way forward with the industry. There is likely to be a further consultation later in the year.

# E. **Mobile and Radio Spectrum**

## Indirect access for mobiles

E.1    Mobile networks are free – but not obliged – to offer Indirect Access (IA) services to their customers. None has so far. In March 1998, a small operator licensed for international services sought indirect access from one of the longer-established mobile networks: the request was refused. The operator therefore asked OFTEL to resolve the dispute under the terms of the Interconnection Directive (ICD).

E.2    A mandatory IA service for mobile networks would be a substantial change affecting customers, providers of alternative services, and the mobile network operators. For consumers there would be expanded choices – and the possibility of reduced prices for calls from mobile (depending on the charges for the use of the mobile network).

E.3    For service providers, IA opens up wider market opportunities in packaging and pricing the services independently of the network operator. For the network operators, IA can provide further marketing opportunities but at the cost of loss of control over their customers and of revenues and profits.

E.4    OFTEL reviewed the issues arising from IA for mobile network during 1998, linking the review with its analysis of competition in the mobile market. This analysis was completed at the end of the year. Consultation documents on both the competitiveness of the mobile market and IA for mobile networks were published in February 1999. OFTEL will publish a statement in June 1999 containing its conclusions from the consultation.

## Fixed mobile integration

E.5    Many approaches to the integration of fixed and mobile services are being developed in UK and abroad. They range from simple combinations of still distinct services through to the ultimate concept of a seamless service – one phone, one number and one bill. The final objective will be to free customers from any restrictions so that they can make calls and others can call them in all situations with a full range of services without caller or called needing to be concerned about the technology involved.

E.6    OFTEL sees its role as one of enabling efficient development of innovative approaches to serving customers – in particular by ensuring that theses market developments are not distorted or blocked by the power exerted by some operators in some markets which might be leveraged into the integrated market or through to other markets. Throughout 1998, OFTEL has been keeping track of this emerging market and the services it offers in UK and abroad. This is in order to assess where regulation may be necessary to ensure fair market opportunities for

efficient providers or may need adaptation to encourage beneficial developments. OFTEL will sum up its conclusions to date in the statement in June on it review of the mobile market.

## Radio spectrum issues

E.7    OFTEL has continued to devote considerable resources to radio spectrum issues over the last year. It has been working with the Radiocommunications Agency (RA) and the DTI to ensure that spectrum allocation policy and the implementation of spectrum pricing proposals promote economically efficient use of the spectrum and reflect the needs of the telecommunications industry and users arising from growth and from the emergence of new technologies, services and customer demands.

E.8    OFTEL's main contribution on radio spectrum issues has been to work with the RA on the development of policy for the third-generation mobile market and for the auction of spectrum early in 2000. In addition OFTEL has been working closely with the RA, providing advice and input on key issues such as broadband access, spectrum trading and administrative pricing.

# F. **Improving Accountability**

## Actions to improve accountability

F.1    In February 1998, OFTEL published a statement, *Improving Accountability – Further Steps.* This announced a series of new measures designed to ensure that it is even more accountable and transparent in the future.

F.2    The initiatives came after a six month consultation with telecommunications customers, consumer groups, the industry and advisory bodies. A consultative document *Improving Accountability – OFTEL's Procedures and Processes* issued in July 1997 had sought the views of consumers, consumer organisations, industry and others about nine actions OFTEL proposed to improve accountability. In preparing its statement, OFTEL took account of the National Consumer Council's code of practice on consultations *Government Consultations: Not Just a Paper Exercise.*

F.3    Responses to the consultation document came from statutory and non-statutory consumer groups, local authorities and the telecommunications industry.

F.4    OFTEL used the responses to its consultation procedure to produce a five-point plan to enhance accountability further. These included debating OFTEL's forward work programme in a consultative meeting; making greater use of OFTEL's website to increase awareness of OFTEL documents; and publishing information on consumer complaints received by OFTEL.

## Performance Measures

F.5    OFTEL seeks continuous improvement to both its performance in addressing competition issues and its case-handling. During 1998, OFTEL's effectiveness in casework handling was the subject of an extensive study by the National Audit Office (NAO). The Public Accounts Committee (PAC) subsequently examined the NAO report. During 1998, the Director General established a review of efficiency and effectiveness of the casework and compliance across OFTEL to encompass preparation for the Competition Act.

F.6    As part of OFTEL's review of casework procedures, the key targets of completing 75% of all investigations within three months and 100% within six months proposed from July 1997 onwards were examined closely. The data gathered by the Compliance Directorate showed that, unless the quality of investigations or the extent of consultations with interested parties were reduced, the three-month target for competition complaints was unrealistic.

F.7    When he gave evidence to the Public Accounts Committee on the NAO report, the Director General emphasised that targets should be realistic and fair to staff and better related to the particular complexities of each individual case. The

Compliance Directorate has since established differential targets for different types of cases, so that those which, because of their complexity, will take longer can be clearly identified at the early stage of full investigation.

F.8    While reverting to its original target of completing 75% of investigations within six months, and all within one year, OFTEL is aiming for good-quality casework and stretching but realistic targets. It will set specific targets for each case. Less complex cases will be set a three month clearance target. Complaints requiring immediate action will be set even a more demanding timescale. OFTEL will continue to monitor its performance against these targets to ensure that its overall performance does not slacken.

## NAO report on OFTEL's effectiveness in casework handling

F.9    The 1997 annual report stated that the NAO was nearing the conclusion of a study of OFTEL's effectiveness in handling casework.

F.10   On 8 April 1998, the NAO published its report, entitled *Countering Anti-Competitive Behaviour in the Telecommunications Industry*. The NAO study carried out an extensive review of OFTEL's effectiveness in identifying and dealing with anti-competitive behaviour. The NAO examined how OFTEL had dealt with 217 competition cases over a three year period (1995-97). An external advisory panel supported the NAO in examining the cases. A survey of companies in the telecommunications market was also commissioned to assess the industry's awareness of OFTEL's role and effectiveness in dealing with anti-competitive behaviour.

F.11   The NAO report reflected the significant advances made by OFTEL in improving the investigation of anti-competitive behaviour and, in particular, that OFTEL is carrying out competition investigation faster. It also noted that the tele-communications industry has greater confidence in the way OFTEL investigates anti-competitive behaviour.

F.12   Amongst its recommendations, the NAO report said that OFTEL should continue to look for further ways to recruit and retain staff with appropriate skills and expertise, and consider further independent review of the quality of its investigations.

F.13   The Director General accepted all the recommendations in the NAO report for improving OFTEL's speed and effectiveness in dealing with anti-competitive behaviour. He said that OFTEL would continue to improve its responsiveness to meet the needs of an increasingly competitive marketplace. However, it is not always easy to reconcile a complainant's desire for a swift decision with the need for OFTEL to carry out a fair and thorough investigation before deciding on enforcement action.

## PUBLIC ACCOUNTS COMMITTEE EXAMINE NAO REPORT

F.14   In June 1998, the Public Accounts Committee examined the NAO report on countering anti-competitive behaviour in the telecommunications industry. The Committee took evidence from the Director General in relation to the NAO report and a number of wider issues affecting the telecommunications market. The Committee's conclusions and recommendations were published in its 64th report on 12 August 1998.

F.15   The Committee examined OFTEL's effectiveness in the investigation of anti-competitive behaviour and the adequacy of its staffing engaged in this work. It also considered the issues affecting competition and customer choice and the impact of the new Competition Act.

F.16   The Committee emphasised that the telecommunications industry is dynamic and that speedy action by OFTEL is essential if anti-competitive behaviour by dominant companies is to be prevented. The Committee also underlined the need for OFTEL to have senior staff with business acumen and urged OFTEL to press on with plans to equip staff with skills and knowledge to be able to employ the new Competition Act effectively. It also observed the need for operators' pricing to be clear and transparent so that consumers might make informed choice. The Committee welcomed OFTEL's efforts to ensure that customers were able to compare prices and looked to OFTEL to act if it found tariffs were anti-competitive or harmed consumer interests.

## FOLLOW-UP TO NAO REPORT

F.17   The Compliance Directorate has already put in place an action plan to address the recommendations made by the NAO. It has also taken steps to address the concerns raised by the Public Accounts Committee hearing.

The measures taken during 1998 were:

- ◆ The Director General established a review of efficiency and effectiveness of the casework and compliance across OFTEL to encompass preparation for Competition Act cases.

- ◆ OFTEL continued to pursue a pro-active approach by initiating investigations itself and by encouraging affected parties to register formal complaints. A project was set up to ensure that the Compliance Directorate pro-actively identifies issues that need investigating. During 1998 24% (1997 10%) of the investigations into anti-competitive behaviour were investigations initiated by OFTEL.

- ◆ As regards staffing, OFTEL has taken steps to improve training of its staff to meet the needs of the regulatory work. Constraints continue to exist in attracting from the private sector. However OFTEL has been able to attract high calibre staff, with outside experience and expertise.

◆ An experienced senior case officer is currently participating in the Office of Fair Trading Competition Act early guidance training.

◆ The Director General has stated that he wants to encourage better and clearer information from telecom companies to help customer be more 'expert' buyers. OFTEL is currently working to provide price comparisons funded by the industry. This information should be published from summer 1999 onwards.

F.18    The conclusions of both the NAO and PAC reports were carefully considered as part of the review of OFTEL's structure. OFTEL remains committed to working through the action plan it submitted to the Committee. The Compliance Directorate is on course for delivering the plan's objectives by March 1999.

## Operational excellence in casework

F.19    Implementing the recommendations of the NAO report on *Countering Anti-competitive Behaviour in the Telecommunications Industry*, together with issues emerging from the new Competition Act, indicated the need for an urgent review to take account of wider issues concerning procedures for compliance activity and casework.

F.20    In June 1998, the Director General established a review of efficiency and effectiveness of the casework and compliance procedures in use across OFTEL. A programme for casework compliance and quality monitoring was set up. The objective of the programme was to develop and introduce robust casework procedures; ensure internal consistency in conducting compliance casework; and develop and operate a process of ongoing compliance and quality monitoring of casework activity.

F.21    OFTEL's new structure based on two operational directorates has assisted in implementation of this programme. The Compliance Directorate is now the focal point of OFTEL's work on enforcing licences and competition legislation and dealing with complaints about anti-competitive behaviour and customer complaints.

F.22    The initial stage of OFTEL's review of casework procedures has been completed and new procedures are being tested. A casework quality monitoring system has been implemented across the directorate and is beginning to provide useful feedback on casework procedures. It is also helping to identify and remedy tensions between conflicting internal priorities and processes.

F.23    An outward looking element of this programme is the establishment of an industry compliance forum which is being developed with the industry to assist telecommunication operators to review proactively compliance programmes within their own organisations.

## Small Business Task Force

F.24   OFTEL's Small Business Task Force, chaired by the Director General, met in March, June and October 1998 and is making good progress in tackling issues of concern to this key group of users for the UK economy. The Task Force, which consists of individuals from small businesses, the telecommunications industry and Government sectors, is working to enable small businesses to get a better deal from telecommunications by identifying and encouraging the provision of targeted and relevant information that allows small businesses to be better purchasers of telecommunications.

F.25   Key developments from the Task Force's work are:

### NTL AND BT TO PROVIDE ISDN2 AVAILABILITY LOCATION INFORMATION

F.26   NTL and BT agreed to develop their Internet websites to show small businesses – and small business advisers and economic development agencies – where they can get fast access to the Internet via basic rate ISDN (ISDN2) services. This information will be available in 1999. This will especially help businesses outside the main urban areas to plan their location decisions and economic development agencies to map telecommunications infrastructure on a similar basis to that used for road and rail links.

### SUPPORT FOR BUYERS' GUIDE AND CODE OF CONDUCT ON INSTALLATION AND MAINTENANCE

F.27   The Task Force will publish a Buyers' Guide to help small businesses when they have telecommunications equipment installed or maintained. A draft guide prepared by Task Force member John Tyreman of the Telecom Users Association (TUA) is to be used as a basis for different versions for the micro business (nine or fewer employees) and other small businesses with ten or more employees.

F.28   The Task Force will also publish a Code of Conduct for telecommunications network operators, installers and maintainers. The code is designed to help small businesses by ensuring that, when several different suppliers are involved, the customer does not find that each supplier is unwilling to take responsibility for problems. The draft code, prepared by Glenn Tookey of Telewest, is being trialled by network operators and telephone equipment maintainer companies.

F.29   The Task Force also supported an initiative backed by the Telecommunications Industry Association (TIA) to introduce a range of licensed professional qualifications for individuals in the fields of telecommunications cabling and equipment installation and maintenance. Small business customers will be encouraged by the Task Force to specify contractors who are quality assured and employ individuals with a relevant European Institute for Telecommunications Engineering (EITE) licence.

F.30 The Task Force is exploring ways of encouraging the dissemination of regularly updated good-practice advice to small businesses on the use of the Internet, including what to look for in terms of quality of service, and the use of other advanced telecommunications services.

F.31 This type of information, together with good-practice advice and information sources emerging from the other Task Force activities described above and from a range of other sources, could most usefully be provided through an actively managed, interactive website. On behalf of the Task Force, OFTEL is looking to encourage relevant private and public organisations and businesses to support and promote a website initiative to do this.

F.32 The Task Force will publish a report in Spring 1999 illustrating areas where it has succeeded in improving the information and advice available to help small businesses become more informed about the purchase of telecommunications.

## Large Business Telecom User Panel

F.33 OFTEL aims to promote competition in telecommunications for the benefit of customers, and therefore needs to hear customers' views about how competition is working. One way it does this is through an informal panel of large business users of telecommunications. The panel meets three or four times each year.

F.34 The panel comprises individuals with responsibility for purchasing telecommunications services for their companies, who can provide feedback on the impact of competition in the UK and overseas telecommunications markets. Panel members come from a wide range of industry sectors. The panel gives OFTEL an opportunity to discuss proposed and existing policies with a group of users who have a specific interest in the rapid development of advanced telecommunications services.

F.35 The panel's activities are reported through *OFTEL News*. The pace of change in telecommunications means companies need frequent reporting of issues covered.

F.36 The main issues covered at the panel meetings in 1998 were:

- how business customers can get telecommunication operators to share ducts carrying telecommunications cables on their sites;
- how developments in numbering will impact on businesses;
- proposed changes in the arrangements for allocating telephone numbers;
- forthcoming changes in number prefixes;

- proposals for changing freephone number prefixes;

- progress on preliminary enquiry regarding the price of national leased lines supplied by BT;

- the impact on businesses of the Telecommunications (Data Protection and Privacy) Regulations;

- the position on the Corporate Advance Pricing Proposal notified by BT.

## Publicity for OFTEL's activities

F.37 National media attention focused on three main areas of OFTEL's work in 1998:

- OFTEL's investigation into the prices of calls to mobiles and the subsequent reference to, and investigation by, the Monopoly and Mergers Commission;

- problems caused by junk faxes and unwanted telesales calls;

- implementation of the National Numbering scheme, in particular changes to area codes in the year 2000 and the proposals for creating more freephone numbers.

F.38 Press conferences on the investigation in the price of calls to mobiles were extremely well attended. The eventual announcements that there would be large reductions in the call prices were warmly greeted. The media also regularly covered the increasing sales of mobile phones and the fact that their usage soared in 1998. Generally, any issue related to mobile phones resulted in intensive media attention. The year ended with another burst of publicity following OFTEL's announcement in December of the introduction of mobile number portability.

F.39 Unwanted telesales calls and junk faxes continued to be a subject of media attention throughout the year, reflecting the level of complaints which also began to be received by the Consumer Representation Section. Senior OFTEL staff appeared on a range of national and local radio and TV programmes to explain how to deal with the problem. Press coverage, both regional and national, of the difficulties caused by junk faxes was also constant in 1998.

F.40 With the launching of The Big Number campaign – an advertising initiative funded by all the telephone companies working together – media interest in the area code changes planned for the year 2000 intensified as the year progressed. The linked issues of proposals to create new freephone numbers and plans to develop the administration of numbering also attracted media interest, notably from the national press. OFTEL began 1998 with an announcement that Coventry would be added to the list of year 2000 area code changes, and this provoked wide coverage by newspapers, radio and TV in the area.

F.41 Statements by the incoming Director General that he believed that consumers have a right to clearer information on pricing and quality of service were widely covered. He was interviewed throughout the year on related topics, such as the need for clearer information about mobile phone tariffs, the cost of using phones in hotel bedrooms, and plans to publish complaints information for customers.

F.42 Media interest was also high in any OFTEL input into broadcasting issues and information-age topics – especially those connected with the Internet and the emergence of pay-as-you-go and subscription-free services. As the year ended, there was wide coverage that OFTEL was seeking to resolve an industry dispute over the formula for Number Translation Services, particularly in regard to lo-call rates, which are being used by the new breed of subscription-free Internet service providers.

F.43 Throughout the year, OFTEL featured in press articles covering the full range of its activities from consumer concerns to complex technical issues. There was a notable increase in regional coverage, which may reflect OFTEL's higher profile in geographic areas that are likely to change code in 2000.

F.44 OFTEL completed its review of the licence of Kingston Communications (KC). This was launched with a press conference in Hull and received extensive coverage. A leaflet explaining the scope of the licence review was distributed throughout libraries in the area. A public meeting was also held in Hull which attracted around 300 residents – many in response to a campaign organised by local media. Although initial local coverage of OFTEL's proposals was hostile, the eventual announcement of the proposals to amend KC's licence was well received and seen as a positive step for the area. The intensive and unusual level of interest in a licence review exercise reflected the special position of KC in the local community.

F.45 A total of 83 OFTEL press releases were published during the year, with a further two on behalf of the Advisory Committees. However, OFTEL's Internet site and the e-mail mailing list are proving to be increasingly useful tools to communicate OFTEL's work to a wider range of groups. Many foreign journalists contacted OFTEL after using the website to find out about the UK telecommunications industry in response to liberalisation of European telecommunications markets.

F.46 OFTEL again participated in the Telecommunications Managers' Association (TMA) exhibition and conference in Brighton. Visitors to the OFTEL stand caught up on the latest regulatory moves and publications. OFTEL staff at all levels spoke throughout the year at a number of seminars and conferences on telecommunications issues to help clarify the organisation's proposals and explain decisions while also seeking input into consultation exercises.

## OFTEL on the Internet

F.47   OFTEL's World Wide Web (WWW) site on the Internet has been up and running since June 1995. The site contains all OFTEL's free-of-charge publications, numbering information (including the full list of allocated codes), a list of licensees, OFTEL's diary, and some general information about OFTEL. There are also hyperlinks to OFTEL's press releases and responses to consultative documents. New publications continued to create particular interest, but the site is also used as a comprehensive source of background material.

F.48   The number of 'hits' to OFTEL's home page in 1998 was **201,485** compared to 88,500 in 1997. This means that for the third year running the number of visitors to OFTEL's website has doubled.

F.49   The work of developing the website has continued, and there are now new areas, including service provider information and networks and interconnection. Also new is a glossary of terms, which has succinct definitions of telecommunications terminology; this has proved very useful to website visitors. There are plans to continue to develop the site, and it is hoped to redesign several aspects during 1999.

F.50   OFTEL is aware of the importance of making information readily available and as quickly as possible. This is one of the reasons that the e-mail notification service was set up. The service notifies subscribers as soon as a new document is posted on to the OFTEL website. It has proved to be very popular, and now has over 4000 subscribers.

F.51   It is possible to subscribe to the list automatically from OFTEL's site using the electronic form. Those who wish to join simply go to OFTEL's home page, click on 'what's new' and follow the link from there to the form. Subscribers can use the same form to amend their details.

F.52   OFTEL encourages respondents to its consultations to publish their responses on their own website whenever possible. Links are then arranged from OFTEL's web site. OFTEL's website is: http://www.oftel.gov.uk.

F.53   The six Advisory Committees on Telecommunications outlined in Part Three of this report now have their own website at: www.acts.org.uk.

**Figure 5:** OFTEL's home page on the internet. http://www.oftel.gov.uk

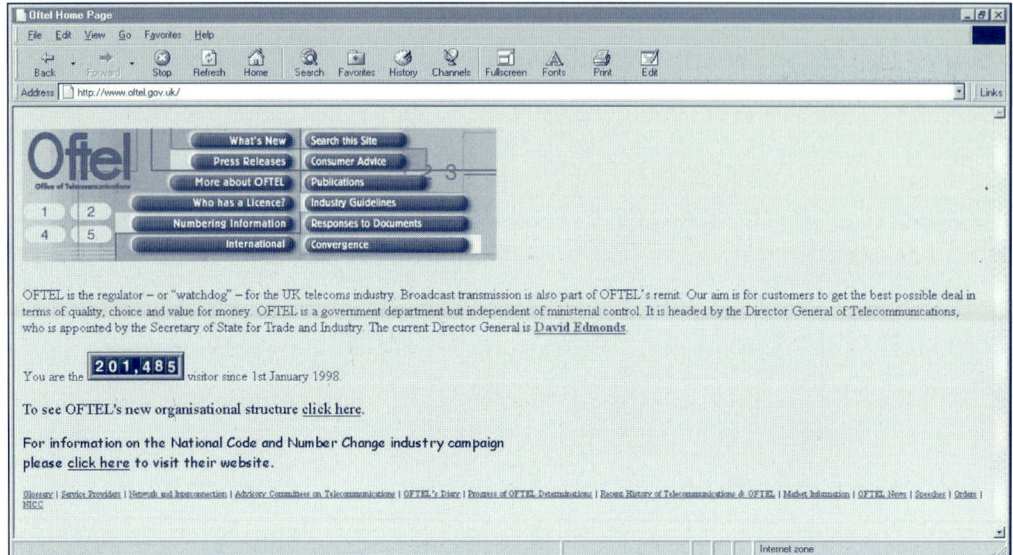

## OFTEL News

F.54 Another important aspect of OFTEL's communications process is the quarterly publication *OFTEL News.* As well as articles by members of the OFTEL staff on the latest developments, and a column by the Director General, the magazine, which has a circulation of 11,000, also covers wider aspects of the telecommunications industry as a whole.

F.55 The magazine contains regular sections on the cable sector, mobile phones and international news, a list of current approvals by the British Approvals Board for Telecommunications; and items of general industry news.

F.56 Topics covered in the four editions in 1998 included number portability and other numbering issues, in particular The Big Number advertising campaign. Also proving very popular is the acronyms section, which each quarter provides an easy reference to some of the jargon that is used in the telecommunications industry.

F.57 Following a survey, a redesign of the magazine took place and was launched with the first issue of 1999, together with new sections and features.

## Research & Intelligence Unit

F.58 The Research & Intelligence Unit (R&I) continues to be the central information point for OFTEL staff and ensures that the provision of services are maintained to:

◆ provide information resources for OFTEL staff and oversee content in the internal electronic information flows, an example of which is OFTEL's Intranet;

- maintain the Public Registrar as required by the 1984 Telecommunication Act;

- maintain an archive of OFTEL publications and distribute hard copies as requested;

- maintain the responses to OFTEL publications;

- manage official Public Records for OFTEL.

F.59  OFTEL's publications and licence information are available from OFTEL's internet site or by contacting the R&I unit by phone, fax, letter or email. On average the R&I unit receive 700 enquiries every month.

## Licences Register

F.60  OFTEL continues to advise the DTI on the granting of new licences. It is important to note that although the DTI issues the licence, it is OFTEL that keeps copies once they have been granted.

F.61  The Licences Register is the repository that contains a copy of every licence granted by the Secretary of State under Section 7 of the 1984 Telecommunications Act. This also includes associated items such as modifications, determinations or the consents that are made by the Director General of OFTEL.

F.62  Within this collection is General Approvals under section 22 of the 1984 Telecommunication Act and a list of standards designated by the Secretary of State under section 22 of the 1984 Telecommunication Act.

F.63  The Register is a substantial source. For example, at the end of 1998 there were 1434 licences (please refer to appendix for Licence Register).

F.64  There has been a moratorium since 1 January 1998 on the granting of certain categories of licence owing to the need to standardise licence conditions under the European Licensing Directive. The moratorium is due to end in June 1999. During 1998 two domestic PTO licences were granted and 45 international facilities licences. By the end of 1998 190 licensees were registered under the international simple voice resale licence.

# G. European and International Activities

## Introduction

G.1 The year 1998 was milestone in the liberalisation of European telecommuni-cations markets. A process that began as long ago as 1984 with cautious, limited liberalisation culminated on 1 January 1998 with the full liberalisation of voice telephony in most EU (European Union) member states. While implementation of the entire package of liberalising measures differed between some member states, the year was greeted with optimism for the future of the industry and the resulting benefits to the European economy.

G.2 A major task for OFTEL during the year was to work with the DTI on the negotiation and implementation of key directives underpinning and advancing the liberalisation programme.

## Licensing Directive

G.3 The Licensing Directive plays a key part in the liberalisation programme. It is designed to create a common framework for telecommunications licences granted by EU member states and to produce a system of licensing that is transparent, objective, proportionate and non-discriminatory. While the UK's regime was already in line with many of the requirements of the directive, certain key changes were required to ensure compatibility.

G.4 The main provisions of the directive were introduced into UK law by the Telecommunications (Licensing) Regulations 1997. The first stage of the directive required all new licences issued from 1 January 1998 to be compliant. Priority was then given to completing the work on the remaining licence templates for new licences to be issued. However, the bulk of licensing activity during the year was work on all licences granted prior to 1 January 1998 to bring them into line with the requirements of the Licensing Directive by the end of the year. Because of the sheer number and variety of licences, this work proved to be an enormous task, and, as a consequence, the UK applied to the European Commission for, and was granted, a deferment until 30 June 1999.

G.5 The UK has issued around 400 individual licences and around 20 class licences since 1984 for a wide range of different telecommunications services. During this time, the regulatory regime has continued to develop, and, as a result, there are a number of variations between licences within the same category of operation. In some cases, differences between licences have given rise to situations in which individual licences have had to be amended in order to avoid discriminatory situations arising between licensees. The task of bringing existing licences into line has also been complicated by the implementation of other directives, such as the Amending Leased Lines Directive, the Interconnection Directive and the Revised Voice Telephony Directive.

G.6   The DTI issued its consultation document on the texts of the various Public Telecommunication Operator (PTO) licences (standard, BT, Kingston Communications, mobile and cable) in November 1998 and on other texts (Telecommunications Services Class Licence, Self Provision Class Licence and ISVR Licence) in December. The consultation period for the PTO licence texts closed on 11 January 1999 and for the others on 21 January. The DTI and OFTEL are considering the comments received. Consultation on the remaining licence texts took place in February 1999.

## Interconnection Directive

G.7   Following implementation of the Interconnection Directive at the end of 1997, OFTEL published a statement *Identification of significant market power for the purposes of the interconnection directive* in February 1998 which explained how the concept has been defined and applied in the UK.

G.8   OFTEL's proposals for granting rights and obligations to interconnect was the subject of a further consultative document *Rights and obligations to interconnect under the EU Interconnection Directive* published in March 1998. The DTI's decision to implement as proposed in the light of consultation was set out in its consultation document on the new PTO licences. An OFTEL statement will be published in April 1999 detailing how the proposals will be given practical effect.

## Voice Telephony and Universal Services Directive

G.9   The Voice Telephony and Universal Services Directive, which came into force in the middle of the year, replaced the existing Voice Telephony Directive (95/62/EC) in the light of full liberalisation from 1 January 1998. OFTEL worked closely with the DTI on the regulations implementing the directive.

G.10  The aim of the directive is to ensure the availability of good-quality fixed public telephone services throughout the EU. It also defines, in the context of universal service, the set of services to which all users should have access at an affordable price. The directive is mainly concerned with fixed telephone operators but also includes some requirements (such as the provision of directory-enquiry services) on mobile operators.

G.11  In accordance with the directive, OFTEL published a statement, *The Principles of Affordability,* in November, setting out how it achieves affordable prices.

G.12  Provisions in the directive set out various obligations on telecommunications companies that give further rights to consumers. The requirements on operators range from offering an entry in the directory-enquiry database to providing itemised bills. These obligations have been incorporated into new licence conditions. For those companies that offer telecommunications services but do not run systems and are therefore unlicensed, there are free-standing regulations that can be enforced by the Director General through court proceedings.

G.13 The directive also imposes additional obligations on operators that are determined as having Significant Market Power (SMP). The requirements on operators with SMP include the need to ensure that retail tariffs are cost-oriented.

G.14 In April, OFTEL published a consultation document, *The Identification of Operators with Significant Market Power for the Application of Detailed Rules under Purposes of the EC Voice Telephony and Universal Services Directive*, setting out its proposed determination. Following consideration of the responses to this document, the Director General determined BT and Kingston Communications as operators with SMP for the purposes of this directive. In October, the Director General published a statement, *Operators with Significant Market Power for the Application of Detailed Rules under Purposes of the EC Voice Telephony and Universal Service Directive*, explaining the reasons for the determination.

## Data Protection and Privacy Directive

G.15 In line with the provisions of the Data Protection and Privacy Directive, OFTEL has worked in three areas to address the data-protection and privacy concerns of consumers. These areas cover:

◆ consumers' rights to choose how they are listed in directories or by a directory-enquiry service. Later in 1999, consumers will be able to choose to have no entry in a directory, to Have no reference to their gender, and/or to have only part of their address listed.

◆ The Code of Practice on the Use of Directory Information. OFTEL and the Data Protection Registrar have worked closely to produce the Code, which is enforceable by the Registrar and sets out what can and cannot be done with directory information. For example, the details that consumers have asked to appear in the phone book cannot be changed without their permission, and directory enquiries may only give out a consumer's number if the enquirer gives a name and an approximate address.

◆ Consumers' rights in relation to unsolicited telephone calls or faxes made or sent for the purpose of direct marketing. OFTEL invited tenders in early 1999 for an organisation to set up and run a scheme allowing consumers to opt out of receiving such calls or faxes. Individuals will be able to put their telephone number on a list of numbers that may not be telephoned for direct-marketing purposes, and individuals and companies will be able to put their fax number on a list of numbers that may not be faxed for direct-marketing purposes. There will be an outright ban on sending such faxes to individuals, but individuals will be able to register on this list as an additional safeguard. Details of this scheme will be widely publicised in 1999.

# Numbering Directive

G.16 From the year 2000, customers of BT and Kingston Communications will be able to have certain call types carried by other operators without, as now, having to dial extra digits. This is called Carrier Preselection (CPS) or equal access, and it is an EU requirement under the Numbering Directive (98/61/EC). Customers will not need to change their BT or Kingston lines and so will still pay these operators for line rental.

G.17 OFTEL consulted widely with the industry and consumer groups on the types of calls that should be subject to CPS requirements. It subsequently set out the final functional specifications for the CPS service in the summer of 1998. Customers will have three options: international calls, national calls, and all calls (excluding emergency calls, operator services and directory enquiries). The first two options may be combined so that customers can preselect the same operator or different operators for national and international calls. Customers will also be able to override their preselection on an individual call by dialling a short code (provided that they have a contract with the relevant indirect-access operator).

G.18 BT will make CPS available to its customers by the end of 2000 for national and international calls, with other calls following around the end of 2001, subject to the European Commission accepting these timescales. The Numbering Directive obliges BT to introduce CPS by 1 January 2000, but substantial software upgrades are first required, and the work has to be meshed in with other software changes currently underway to make BT's network millennium-compliant. Kingston customers will have all CPS call types available from the start of 2000. Other operators with directly connected customers do not have to offer CPS on their networks, but they may decide to do so.

G.19 The UK industry, consumer groups and OFTEL have been cooperating from early 1998 to develop standard CPS processes (for example, order handling, faults and billing) and consumer-protection measures, including a code of practice for CPS operators and robust procedures to avoid 'slamming' – a change of operator or service without the customer's knowledge or consent.

G.20 OFTEL formally consulted in November on how charges for CPS should be set. It set out its conclusions in February 1999.

G.21 The Numbering Directive outlined in this report also includes provisions concerning number portability.

## Radio Equipment and Telecommunications Terminal Equipment (RTTE)

G.22 As anticipated in the 1997 annual report, a common position on the Draft Directive on Radio Equipment and Telecommunications Terminal Equipment (RTTE) was reached under the UK Presidency in June 1998. By the end of 1998, agreement had been reached on a joint text approved by the Conciliation Committee. It is likely that the Directive will enter into force in April 1999 and be implemented in April 2000. The DTI will be issuing a consultation document on UK regulations required to comply with the Directive in Autumn 1999.

G.23 The directive will replace the Telecommunications Terminal Equipment (TTE) Directive (98/13/EC). It extends the scope of the previous directive unambiguously to all radio communications equipment, streamlines the current lengthy procedure for type approval through Common Technical Regulations by allowing compliance with the directive's essential requirements to be demonstrated by manufacturers' declarations. It also reduces the number of essential requirements with which most products have to comply. Apart from its involvement in the negotiation of the directive, OFTEL played a significant role in the work of *ad hoc* groups formed by the European Commission to carry out preliminary work on implementing the directive. OFTEL provided the chairman for the group working on the publication of interface specifications and contributed to another group's consideration of the applicability of the essential requirement for users with a disability.

## EU legislation under negotiation

### DRAFT DIRECTIVE ON ELECTRONIC COMMERCE

G.24 The Draft Directive on Electronic Commerce covers general e-commerce issues such as liability for illegal content (including copyright infringement), advertising, electronic contracts and professional standards. It favours the so-called 'country of origin' principle, under which online service providers established in an EU member state would be subject to rules in that country rather than in the country of residence of the consumer. It also introduces a 'mere conduit' defence for online service providers and operators whose networks or facilities are used for illegal activities without their knowledge or consent. Negotiations on this proposal started at the end of 1998 and are expected to continue for some time. It is not yet clear how far it will affect OFTEL.

### DRAFT DIRECTIVE ON ELECTRONIC SIGNATURES

G.25 The Draft Directive on Electronic Signatures seeks to establish a common legal framework for electronic signatures (a method of authenticating electronic documents) in order to promote trade in the Single Market. In particular, it harmonises the requirements for Certification Service Providers (CSPs-trusted third parties who will be responsible for administrating a voluntary scheme certifying the authenticity of organisations seeking to benefit from using electronic signatures). It also seeks to bring the same level of legal recognition to electronic signatures as currently exists for physical ones. Negotiations during the year failed to reach agreement, so it is now likely that this directive will be adopted early in 2000.

DRAFT DIRECTIVE ON THE SEPARATION OF CABLE TV NETWORKS

G.26 The Draft Directive on the Separation of Cable TV Networks is aimed at enforcing structural separation between the traditional telecommunications network of dominant operators and any cable television networks that they may own. It is expected that the European Commission will adopt the directive under article 90 of the Treaty of Rome in the first half of 1999, but it only applies to certain categories of cable operator, and it appears that no UK operators fall within these.

## 1999 Review

G.27 In March 1998, OFTEL responded to the European Commission's Green Paper on the convergence of the telecommunications, media and information-technology sectors. It was made clear that the majority of the issues raised would be taken forward in the context of the 1999 review of the EU communications regulatory framework. This fundamental review springs as much from the effective implementation of the liberalisation package as from increasing convergence, and OFTEL is keen to involve as many players and interested parties in the UK as possible. Towards the end of 1998, OFTEL and the DTI convened a small group of individuals from the communications sector (the 1999 Policy Review Focus Group) to contribute to the debate on the future of regulation. This group will continue to meet during 1999, a crucial year in the process of influencing Europe on future policy in the sector.

G.28 In the meantime, the European Commission has launched a number of studies into telecommunications regulation and the state of the single telecommunications market. These, alongside a Commission paper on regulatory principles and objectives, will feed into a consultation document to be issued towards the end of the 1999. The entire review process is likely to culminate in the adoption of new legislation around 2003.

G.29 The 1999 review was recognised as a project in its own right within OFTEL in 1998, and this will continue into 1999.

## Other policy developments

RADIO SPECTRUM POLICY GREEN PAPER

G.30 OFTEL is working with the Radiocommunications Agency to prepare a response to this European Commission Green Paper, presented during the year, on the efficient use of the radio spectrum.

RECOMMENDATIONS ON INTERCONNECTION IN A LIBERALISED
TELECOMMUNICATIONS MARKET, PARTS I AND II (98/195/EC AND 98/322/EC

G.31 These provided guidance to National Regulatory Authorities (NRAs) on interconnection charges based on best current-practice measures for use when assessing the charges for interconnection proposed by operators with specific obligations in this area. This was thought to be necessary pending the implementation of forward-looking, long-run average incremental cost measures for determining charges across all member states. A further recommendation later in the year (98/511/EC) amended these best current practice charges. These regulations also gave guidance to NRAs on the implementation of accounting-separation and cost-accounting systems by operators designated as having SMP.

### NOTICE ON THE APPLICATION OF COMPETITION RULES TO ACCESS AGREEMENTS IN THE TELECOMMUNICATIONS SECTOR (OJ C 265, 22/8/98, PAGES C265/2 – C265/28)

G.32 This covers a range of issues that the Director General must consider when taking action under the Competition Act. These include the interaction between telecommunications-specific rules and articles 85 and 86 of the Treaty of Rome, which proscribe anti-competitive behaviour and abuse of a dominant position; economic issues such as the definition of markets and essential facilities; and regulatory issues such as accounting principles and the relationship between SMP and dominance.

## International contacts

G.33 OFTEL takes part in and contributes to a wide range of international organisations and groups. The most important of these are described in this section. Details of others can be found at the end of this section.

### INDEPENDENT REGULATORS' GROUP

G.34 The Independent Regulators' Group (IRG) brings together the heads of the independent NRAs of western Europe. The group's purpose is to improve links between the different NRAs, discuss issues of mutual concern and encourage the exchange of experience and best practice. It is currently looking at issues including cross-border interconnection (OFTEL hosted two workshops on this in January and June), how to determine SMP under the terms of various directives and the practicalities of exchanging information between NRAs. It operates in three different ways: through biannual meetings of the heads, through official-level working groups, and through information exchange. The fourth meeting of the IRG has been hosted by OFTEL in March 1999.

### HIGH-LEVEL COMMITTEE OF TELECOMMUNICATIONS REGULATORY AUTHORITIES

G.35 The High-Level Committee of Telecommunications Regulatory Authorities, chaired by the European Commission, met once during the year, in Vienna in September as the guest of the Austrian regulator. There is a trend toward moving the Committee to discuss more substantive policy issues than previously. Mobile interconnection regulation and electronic-commerce issues were both discussed during the year. The Contact Forum – a meeting with administrations from central and eastern Europe – was a well received innovation that took place immediately before the Vienna meeting.

## EUROPEAN TELECOMMUNICATIONS STANDARDS INSTITUTE

G.36 The European Telecommunications Standards Institute (ETSI) has the main responsibility for the pan-European production of voluntary telecommunications standards and the technical aspects of European telecommunications regulatory measures (including input to mandatory standards under Directive 98/13/EC). During the year, OFTEL's technical experts contributed actively to the work of ETSI's Analogue Terminals and Access (ATA) Project and the Telecommunications and Internet Protocol Harmonisation over Networks (TIPHON) project.

G.37 The ATA project has primarily addressed the harmonisation of requirements for approvals for analogue terminal equipment (for example, simple telephones and modems). ATA laid the technical foundations for Common Technical Requirement (CTR) 21 and CTR 38, which were adopted during the year, and for interim CTR 37, which will be adopted in early 1999. This will enable pan-European approval of non voice and voice apparatus and so bring the benefits of harmonisation to consumers and the industry.

G.38 The TIPHON project has been active in various fields. Those of particular interest to OFTEL are service interoperability, charging/billing, numbering, calling-line identification and access to the emergency services. There is worldwide interest in this work, not only from telecommunications organisations but also from the IT industry.

G.39 OFTEL also monitors the work of other ETSI committees, especially those working in the areas of third-generation mobile communications and the forthcoming Radio & Telecommunications Terminal Equipment (RTTE) Directive.

## OTHER INTERNATIONAL CONTACTS

G.40 OFTEL continued to be a popular destination for regulatory colleagues from around the world. Heads of NRAs from France, Germany, Switzerland, Singapore and Australia visited, and OFTEL's Director General held meetings in the United States with a variety of industry players in that market in the spring. More than 100 international meetings were held at working level during the year, including full bilaterals with the German, Swedish and Norwegian regulatory authorities.

G.41 An increasingly important part of OFTEL's international work is outreach to the countries of Central and Eastern Europe as they attempt to adopt the acquis of European Union legislation in telecommunications. OFTEL experts contributed to seminars on liberalisation and licensing in Hungary and Slovakia, while OFTEL and its partners in the Independent Regulators' Group of European regulatory authorities were preparing a mission to Poland as the year ended.

## General Agreement on Trades in Services (GATS)

G.42 The General Agreement on Trades and Services (GATS) telecommunications protocol entered into force on 5 February 1998. Applying the obligations of the GATS to telecommunications, the protocol should ensure that markets are opened to all World Trade Organisation (WTO) member countries on a non-discriminatory basis as they are progressively liberalised. The protocol had little effect on the UK's own domestic regime as its principles were already embodied in the existing regulatory and market framework.

## Other international organisations and groups

### OPEN NETWORK PROVISION COMMITTEE

G.43 The Open Network Provision (ONP) Committee is a standing committee of administrations of EU member states with provision for industry and consumer bodies to attend as observers. It advises the European Commission on the development of the ONP programme, which includes the most important harmonisation directives such as the Interconnection Directive and the Licensing Directive. The Committee meets about every two months. Meetings during the year looked at issues such as cross-border interconnection and universal service. The 1999 review of communications regulation now underway in the EU will occupy more of the ONP Committee's time in 1999.

### EUROPEAN COMMITTEE FOR TELECOMMUNICATIONS REGULATORY AFFAIRS

G.44 The main purpose of the European Committee for Telecommunications Regulatory Affairs (ECTRA) is to be a meeting-point for both telecommunications regulatory authorities and ministries responsible for telecommunications affairs from the member countries of the European Conference of Postal and Telecommunications Administrations (CEPT). Much of its work is devolved to subgroups, in which OFTEL continued to participate during the year. OFTEL chairs the accounting principles and interconnection (APRII) subgroup and participates in the subgroup on numbering.

### APPROVALS COMMITTEE FOR TERMINAL EQUIPMENT

G.45 The Approvals Committee for Terminal Equipment (ACTE) is the advisory committee to the European Commission established under the Telecommunications Terminal Equipment Directive (98/13/EC). As well as offering general guidance on the application of the directive, it has formal responsibility for recommending the adoption of CTRs, which are harmonised technical standards binding on all EU

Member States. During the year, 19 new or revised CTRs were adopted, including seven relating to satellite communications, two to ISDN packet mode and one to in-flight telephony (TFTS).

G.46 However, far and away the most important was the long-awaited CTR 21 for analogue non voice access to the public switched telephone network. This was supplemented by CTR 38, for analogue handset telephony, and by ACTE's recommendation in December 1998 that the Commission adopt an interim CTR 37 for analogue voice access to the PSTN. The effect of these CTRs will be to bring consumers the advantages, for the first time, of a single market for terminals capable of accessing the analogue PSTN.

G.47 In its role as expert adviser to the UK delegation, OFTEL attended the four ACTE meetings held during the year. However ACTE's activities are now winding down in anticipation of the RTTE Directive, which is expected to enter into force from the start of 2000, and only two meetings have been scheduled for 1999.

## TECHNICAL REGULATIONS APPLICATIONS COMMITTEE

G.48 The Technical Regulations Applications Committee (TRAC) has a broad membership drawn from NRAs, PTOs, manufacturers, test laboratories and Notified Bodies (which are authorised to issue approvals recognised by all member states of the European Union). It plays an important role in advising the European Commission on technical and regulatory matters arising from the implementation of the Telecommunications Terminal Equipment Directive. It also drafts statements that identify the equipment, and the particular features thereof, to which CTRs apply as well as reviewing CTRs delivered by ETSI before passing them on to ACTE . Additionally, it has formed a number of Type Approval Advisory Boards (TAABs) to produce Advisory Notes on the interpretation of CTRs to assist test laboratories and Notified Bodies in their work. TAABs are active in the areas of analogue, DECT, GSM 900 and 1800, ISDN and TETRA.

G.49 TRAC also maintains a list of designated laboratories notified for conformance testing against CTRs. OFTEL participated in the four plenary TRAC meetings held during the year.

# H. Interconnection, Interoperability and Licensing

## Interconnection and Interoperability

H.1   In April 1998, OFTEL published its statement, *Interconnection and Interoperability of Services over Telephony Networks.* The statement explained the conclusions of the consultative exercise on interconnection and interoperability, and set out OFTEL's plans for the implementation of policy. Consultation on this issue included extensive industry discussion at the Interconnection Policy Forum (IPF – now the Operator Policy Forum – see below) and an IPF focus group established specifically for the purpose, as well as and public consultation through a consultative document, *Interconnection and Interoperability: A Framework for Competing Networks,* published in April 1997.

H.2   The statement included:

- a draft new licence condition containing requirements for publication of technical interface specifications by fixed network operators. The condition was subsequently added to relevant licences through implementation of Article 11.2 of the Revised Voice Telephony Directive (RVTD) in the UK;

- draft guidelines on how and when OFTEL will expect to enforce availability of services for interconnection. These guidelines will be published formally in 1999 following further discussion with the industry.

## Interface Control

H.3   The licence condition includes provision for the Director General to determine that an operator has 'Interface Control'. Interface Control is the ability of an operator adversely to affect competition by influencing the costs and timescales involved in the adoption of interfaces by other operators and equipment manufacturers. Determination that an operator has Interface Control has the effect of requiring that operator to consult on proposed new interface specifications prior to publication. The statement signalled OFTEL's intention to determine that BT has Interface Control. The determination was not completed in 1998 but was made in January 1999.

## Determinations

H.4   Three interconnection determinations were made during the year. These were the *Determinations of Charges for BT's Standard Services for the year ending 31 March 1997* and for the six months to 30 September 1998 and the *Determination of Charges for International Private Leased Circuits for the years 1995/96 and 1996/97.*

## Determination as to CWC's status as a Well Established Operator

H.5   OFTEL has a responsibility to ensure that changes in market conditions arising through increased competition and growing liberalisation are reflected in the regulatory regime.

H.6   With this in mind, in December 1998 the Director General made a Determination revising the status of Cable and Wireless status as a Well Established Operator (WEO). This followed an extensive review of CWC's position across all international routes in the market for international retail services and the market for international services to other operators.

H.7   A WEO is an operator with market power, ie the ability to raise price above the competitive level for a non-transitory period of time without losing sales to such a degree as to make this unprofitable. A WEO determination carries with it price publication requirements and a prohibition on undue preference or discrimination.

H.8   The Determination made in December 1998 lifts CWC's WEO status in both markets on 157 routes and in the market for international retail services on a further eight routes; the Determination also lists the 63 countries in respect of which CWC remains Well Established in both markets.

H.9   The main effect of the Determination is that, in respect of the 157 routes referred to above, CWC does not need to publish its prices either for international services to other operators or for international retail services.

## The review of the licences of Kingston Communications (Hull) plc and Kingston Upon Hull City Council

H.10   The consultation document *Delivering the Benefits of the Information Age to Customers in Hull* was published on 2 March 1998. The consultation document set out OFTEL's views on the need to amend the regulatory framework for Kingston Communications and explained how European legislation was also changing the regulatory rules. Key proposals included a recommendation that BT be allowed to operate in the Hull area if it applied for a licence.

H.11   A public meeting was held in Hull on 25 March, chaired by the Director General. The meeting was attended by almost 300 people. The Director General gave a presentation, which was followed by questions from the floor. Many of the questions and comments focused on concerns about the effects of allowing BT to operate in the Hull area. The Director General assured those attending the meeting that appropriate safeguards would be applied to BT's activities in the Hull market.

H.12   There were over 500 written responses to the consultation. On 31 July, OFTEL published its statement on the *Review of the Telecommunications Act Licences of Kingston Communications (Hull) plc and Kingston upon Hull City Council*. The statement analysed the responses to the consultation and set out the

following conclusions:

- ◆ Kingston Communications should be allowed to convey cable television services in Hull (it will need a separate licence to do this);

- ◆ Kingston Communications should be allowed to operate elsewhere in the UK, subject only to basic regulatory constraints;

- ◆ OFTEL will advise the DTI that BT should be allowed to operate in Hull subject to safeguards to prevent anti-competitive behaviour;

- ◆ no retail price control is necessary on Kingston Communications' charges to residential and business customers.

H.13 A number of changes will have to be made during 1999 to Kingston's licence in order to ensure that the schedule of conditions complies with the requirements of the Licensing Directive. These changes will be made by DTI by Regulations laid before Parliament.

## Extension of the licence condition to other licences

H.14 In 1999, it is intended that the new licence condition be included in the licences of the mobile network operators through implementation of the Licensing Directive in the UK. The Directive will consolidate and replace existing licence conditions covering Alterations to the Applicable Systems and Customer Interface Standards. This was explained fully in the April 1998 statement, *Interconnection and Interoperability of Services over Telephony Networks.*

## The Network Futures Group

H.15 OFTEL's Annual Report for 1997 explained that an industry group – the Interconnect Advisory Group (IAG) – had been established to discuss generic interconnection and interoperability matters, with a brief to provide advice to OFTEL and the industry. The IAG continued its programme of work during 1998, and gave itself a new title, the Network Futures Group (NFG) to reflect its functions. Dr Keith Monserrat of Scottish Telecom continued in the role of Chairman of the NFG.

## The Operator Policy Forum

H.16 The Operator Policy Forum (OPF) (formerly the Interconnect Policy Forum) was established by OFTEL for the purpose of briefings and discussions with the industry on topics of general interest to network operating.

H.17 The OPF held eight meetings during 1998/99, at which a number of key issues were presented and discussed. Focus groups were established to address issues that could not be immediately resolved, and all these continue to operate. The issues concerned were:

- Internet traffic management;

- Volatile traffic management;

- Non-geographic number portability;

- Mobile number portability;

- Interconnection charging for Number Translation Services;

- Carrier preselection Commercial Group.

## Network Charge Controls

H.18 OFTEL's Annual Report for 1997 included details of the introduction of new arrangements for the regulation of interconnection charges. These new arrangements – the Network Charge Controls (NCC) – came into effect on 1 October 1997 and will run until 30 September 2001. The controls work as follows:

- Competitive services (ie services that were competitive at the start of the controls) are free of direct charge controls. New network services introduced by BT are presumed to be competitive, but there are provisions in BT's licence for controls to be applied to them if necessary.

- Prospectively competitive services (ie those that are expected to become competitive during the life of the controls) are individually subject to 'safeguard caps' set at RPI+0%.

- Non-competitive services (ie those that will not be competitive during the life of the charge controls) are controlled in three separate baskets subject to charge caps set at RPI-8%.

H.19 At the end of the first charge control year, on 30 September 1998, BT had fulfilled its obligations to reduce network charges in each separate basket of non-competitive services by RPI-8%. Indeed, it did slightly better than its obligations. Overall, non-competitive interconnection charges decreased by more than £16million.

H.20 On 31 December 1998, BT proposed the charge changes required for it to fulfil its obligations in the second charge control year. If they become effective, these proposals will bring about further decreases in excess of £42million in interconnection charges for non-competitive services.

## Network Charge Change Notices

H.21 Under the new arrangements, BT publishes new or changed network charges through publication of a Network Charge Change Notice (NCCN). NCCNs for competitive and prospectively competitive services must be published 28 days before the charge takes effect. NCCNs for non-competitive services must be published 90 days before the charge takes effect. BT published 80 NCCNs during 1998.

## The Network Interoperability Consultative Committee

H.22 The Network Interoperability Consultative Committee (NICC) is a leading UK telecommunications industry forum, originally established in 1992, which deals with the technical issues associated with network competition. It produces voluntary technical specifications on behalf of the UK telecommunications industry and is a source of advice to the Director General. NICC's membership includes representatives of network operators, public exchange manufacturers, terminal equipment suppliers, service providers and users

H.23 During 1998, NICC study groups continued their on-going work on a range of issues, such as IUP (Interconnect User Part) and ISUP (ISDN User Part) signalling, Number Portability, SDH Interconnect, and V5 interface mapping requirements. New studies were initiated on DSL (Digital Subscriber Line), the Interface to the Directory Enquiry Database, and ATM (Asynchronous Transfer Mode) services.

H.24 A particularly important NICC study in 1998 concerned the preparation of a set of guidelines for all UK network operators relating to the publication of the technical characteristics of the network operators' customer interfaces. Publication of these interfaces is a requirement under Directive 98/10/EC, the Revised Voice Telephony Directive (RVTD). Another NICC study group produced the *Voluntary code of practice on call answering and charging arising from the attachment of private equipment and systems to the public switched network.*

H.25 In November, the latest in the series of NICC Open Forums was held in London. These annual events provide opportunities for NICC members and other delegates from the telecommunications community to discuss developing issues in the telecommunications field. This year the themes of the Open Forum centred on access and distribution networks and on the continuing developments in convergence.

# I. **Managing OFTEL's Resources**

## Financial affairs and statement of accounts

I.1    OFTEL's funding is provided by Parliament and is subject to cash limits and running costs control, but it's full costs are recouped from licence fees paid by the operators and from other miscellaneous income. OFTEL's total net expenditure in the financial year ending March 1998 was £10.6 million including £353,000 in respect of end-year flexibility and to fund new work, including an important numbering project (see Memorandum Trading Account). Corresponding expenditure figures for 1996/97 and 1995/96 were £9.6 million and £9.5 million.

I.2    A Statement of Accounts (see **table 8**) for 1997/98 is shown on the next page. **Figure 6** shows how OFTEL's expenditure was divided in 1997/98 between the main areas within OFTEL. Advisory Committee expenditure is included under Consumer Affairs. Staff pay costs accounted for some 55% of total expenditure.

## Audit

I.3    OFTEL's Appropriation Account is audited by the National Audit Office (NAO) and the opinion of the Comptroller and Auditor General for the year ended 31 March 1998 is included in the Statement of Accounts. Staff of the Office of Fair Trading (OFT) provide OFTEL with an internal audit service.

## Prompt payment

I.4    Based on sample surveys of invoices (not including staff claims) settled in April 97 to March 98, OFTEL settled 97% of its undisputed invoices within 30 days of receipt or within contractual terms stated on the invoice. The corresponding figures for 1996/97 and 1995/96 were 96% and 95% respectively. Payment performance is calculated using Treasury guidelines.

**Figure 6:** Division of OFTEL's budget as percentages – 1997/98

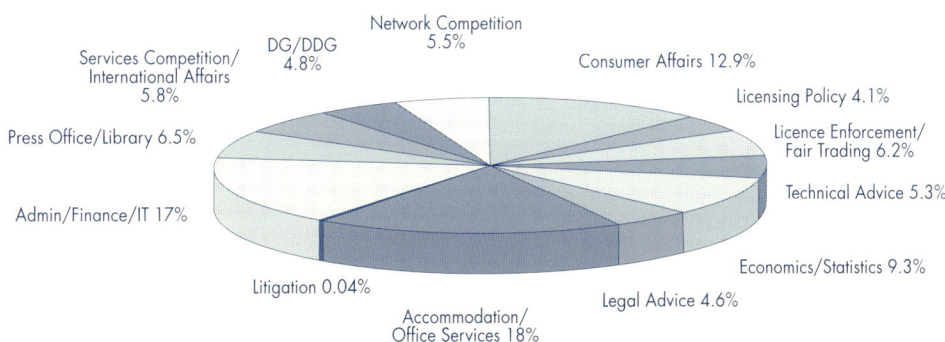

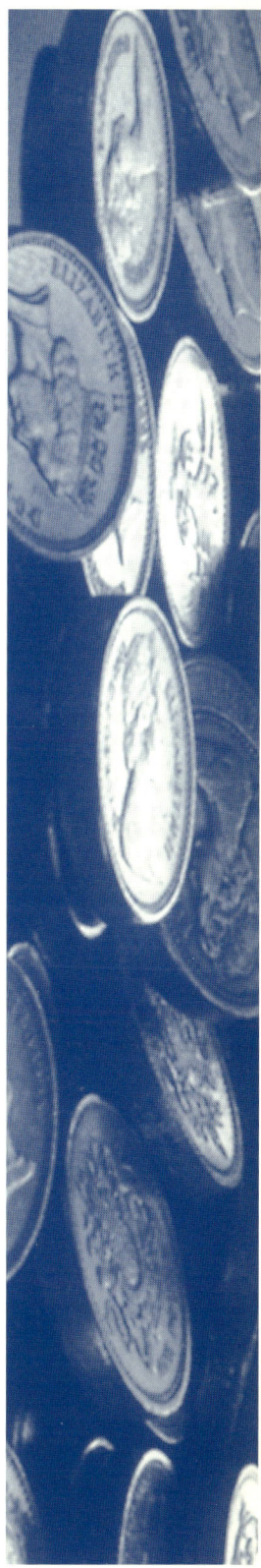

Network Competition 5.5%
DG/DDG 4.8%
Consumer Affairs 12.9%
Services Competition/ International Affairs 5.8%
Licensing Policy 4.1%
Press Office/Library 6.5%
Licence Enforcement/ Fair Trading 6.2%
Admin/Finance/IT 17%
Technical Advice 5.3%
Economics/Statistics 9.3%
Litigation 0.04%
Legal Advice 4.6%
Accommodation/ Office Services 18%

Table 8

# STATEMENT OF ACCOUNTS

## A. Appropriation account statement for the year ended 31 March 1998

Statement of expenditure and appropriations in year.

|  | Grant £'000 | Expenditure £'000 | Variance £'000 |
|---|---|---|---|
| Running Costs | 10,346 | 10,107 | -239 |
| Other Current Expenditure | 285 | 154 | -131 |
| Capital Expenditure | 154 | 394 | +240 |
| **Gross total** | **10,785** | **10,655** | **-130** |
| Less: |  |  |  |
| Appropriations | 24 | 33 |  |
| **Net total** | **10,761** | **10,622** |  |

Account approved on 23 September 1998

**David Edmonds**
Accounting Officer

**Opinion of the Comptroller and Auditor General to the House of Commons**

In my opinion:

* the appropriation account properly presents the expenditure and receipts of Class IV, Vote 8 for the year ended 31 March 1998; and

* in all material respects the expenditure and receipts have been applied to the purposes intended by Parliament and conform to the authorities which govern them.

**John Bourn**
Comptroller and Auditor General
8 October 1998

National Audit Office
157-197 Buckingham Palace Road
Victoria, London SW1W 9SP

## B. Memorandum trading account for the year ended 31 March 1998

| INCOME | Note | £'000 |
|---|---|---|
| ◆ Licence Fees | 2,3 | 10,684 |
| ◆ Other Income | 2,4 | 405 |
| **Total income** |  | **11,089** |
| **EXPENDITURE** |  |  |
| ◆ Staff Related | 2,5 | 6,363 |
| ◆ Accommodation | 6 | 1,706 |
| ◆ Office Supplies | 7 | 229 |
| ◆ Stationery/Consumables | 8 | 113 |
| ◆ Common Services | 9 | 613 |
| ◆ Consultancy | 2 | 938 |
| ◆ Press and Publicity |  | 381 |
| ◆ Library | 10 | 65 |
| ◆ Legal | 11 | 13 |
| ◆ Advisory Committees |  | 150 |
| ◆ Insurance | 12 | 5 |
| ◆ Depreciation | 13 | 272 |
| ◆ Interest on Capital | 14 | 39 |
| ◆ Interest Receivable | 15 | -321 |
| **Total Expenditure** |  | **10,566** |
| **SURPLUS/(DEFICIT)** |  | **523** |

# Notes to the Memorandum Trading Account at 31 March 1998

## 1. Statement of Accounting Policies

**(a)** Preparation of Accounts
The Accounts are prepared under the historic cost convention, modified to include an up to date valuation of assets. They comply, where appropriate, to Statements of Standard Accounting Practice (SSAPs) and Financial Reporting Standards.

**(b)** Depreciation
Depreciation is provided on all tangible fixed assets over an expected life of 5 years on a straight line basis. Assets are revalued using specific indices before calculating depreciation.

A full year's depreciation is charged in the period of purchase.

**(c)** Stocks
Stocks are valued at the lower of cost and net realisable value.

## 2. Supplementary Estimates

One supplementary estimate of £353,000 was obtained by Oftel to carry forward end-year flexibility and to fund new work. This allowed an important Numbering project to proceed resulting in higher administration costs. An additional licence fee of £353,000 was requested in January 1998.

## 3. Licence Fees

| Calculated as follows: | £,000 |
|---|---|
| ◆ received during 1997/98 | 10,677 |
| ◆ less outstanding 1996/97 receipts | 5 |
| ◆ add accrued income at 31 March 1998 | 2 |
| | **10,684** |

Of the above total, £6,811,000 was received from British Telecom, and the remainder from other renewal fees for licences required by statute.

## 4. Other Income

| Calculated as follows: | £,000 |
|---|---|
| ◆ VAT | 312 |
| ◆ Sale of publications | 33 |
| ◆ Miscellaneous receipts | 60 |
| | **405** |

## 5. Employee Information

| (a) Staff Costs | £,000 |
|---|---|
| ◆ Salaries and Wages | 4,725 |
| ◆ ERNIC | 380 |
| ◆ Superannuation | 698 |
| ◆ Secondees | 217 |
| ◆ Hire of Agency staff | 88 |
| ◆ Travel, Subsistence and other payments | 255 |
| | **6,363** |

**(b)** Director General's Remuneration
The Director General's pre-tax earnings as at 31 March 1998 were £141,748.

**(c)** Other Senior Staff
The salaries of the other members of the Senior Management Team were in the following bands:

| | |
|---|---|
| Below £39,999 | 0 |
| £40,000 – £44,999 | 2 |
| £45,000 – £49,999 | 2 |
| £50,000 – £54,999 | 0 |
| £55,000 – £59,999 | 2 |
| £60,000 – £64,999 | 1 |
| £65,000 – £69,999 | 3 |
| £70,000 – £74,999 | 1 |

Salaries include allowances and bonuses paid during the year.

**(d)** Pensions
Employees are covered by the provisions of the Principal Civil Service Pension Scheme, which is non-contributory. Liability for future payments is a charge on the Consolidated Fund. Contributions were paid to the Paymaster General at the rate determined by the Government Actuary and advised by the Treasury.

### 6. Accommodation
This includes rent to Crown Prosecution Service (the major occupier) and other accommodation running costs.

### 7. Office Supplies
This includes such items as postage, telecommunications and maintenance of office equipment.

### 8. Stationery/Consumables
This includes the purchase of stock and small office supplier.

### 9. Common Services
Expenditure incurred for the benefit of the whole office is included under this heading. For example, expenditure by the Finance and Personnel units, canteen services and annual subscriptions.

### 10. Library
Comprises the cost of publications together with associated expenditure.

### 11. Legal
| | £,000 |
|---|---|
| ◆ Legal Fees | 9 |
| ◆ Litigation costs | 4 |
| | 13 |

### 12. Insurance

| Calculated as follows: | £ |
|---|---|
| ◆ 0.1% of Salaries | 4,725 |
| ◆ 0.1% of Stocks (£5,000) | 5 |
| ◆ 0.1% of Fixed Assets | 653 |
| | **5,383** |

### 13. Depreciation

**CALCULATION OF DEPRECIATION AND INTEREST ON CAPITAL (ACTUAL OUTTURN):**

| | 93/94 £ | 94/95 £ | 95/96 £ | 96/97 £ | 97/98 £ |
|---|---|---|---|---|---|
| **Purchases** | 186,151 | 239,527 | 223,474 | 251,472 | 393,469 |
| **Replacement value:** | | | | | |
| of 93/94 purchases | 186,151 | 191,588 | 196,766 | 203,239 | 209,323 |
| of 94/95 purchases | | 239,527 | 246,001 | 254,093 | 261,699 |
| of 95/96 purchases | | | 223,474 | 230,825 | 237,735 |
| of 96/97 purchases | | | | 251,472 | 267,520 |
| of 97/98 purchases | | | | | 393,469 |
| **Total replacement value of capital assets** | | | | | 1,369,746 |
| **Depreciation:** | | | | | |
| of 93/94 purchases | 37,230 | 38,318 | 39,353 | 40,648 | **41,865** |
| of 94/95 purchases | | 47,905 | 49,200 | 50,819 | **52,340** |
| of 95/96 purchases | | | 44,695 | 46,165 | **47,547** |
| of 96/97 purchases | | | | 50,294 | **51,800** |
| of 97/98 purchases | | | | | **78,694** |
| **Total** | | | | | 272,245 |
| **Total capital assets = Total replacement value – Total depreciation to date of existing assets** | | | | | 652,874 |
| **Interest on capital (6%)** | | | | | 39,172 |

**Note**: Phased introduction of current method of calculating depreciation, from 1993/94

### 14. Interest on Capital
Interest on Capital employed is charged at 6% of the total capital employed (defined as Total replacement value of capital assets minus Total depreciation to date of existing assets).

### 15. Interest Receivable
Notional interest on income is calculated by applying the 6% real interest rate to half the total licence fee income, reflecting the fact that the bulk of OFTEL's income is received at the start of the financial year. Fee income received at the start of the year is therefore being treated as negative Working Capital.

## Staffing

I.5    The average number of staff employed in 1997/98 was 166.5. By December 1998 a total of 176 staff were employed in the following groups:

- ◆ Senior staff (Band C and above including professional and technical)   47.6
- ◆ Other professional and technical staff (Band B)                       6.0
- ◆ Executive staff (Band B)                                             79.7
- ◆ Secretarial and administrative support staff (Band B and A)          42.7

I.6    **Figure 7** shows the distribution of staff across the different directorates in OFTEL as at 1 December 1998. Staff in post each year from April 1996 to April 1998 were 160.2, 160.5 and 169.4 respectively.

I.7    Staff of the OFT's Consultancy Inspection and Review Unit provided a job evaluation service to OFTEL.

## Recruitment

I.8    Recruitment in OFTEL is carried out on the basis of fair and open competition and selection on merit in accordance with the Recruitment Code laid down by the Civil Service Commissioners. There are internal checks in place to ensure that all recruitment is carried out in accordance with the Recruitment Code. In addition, OFTEL is subject to an independent Recruitment Adequacy and Compliance Audit carried out on behalf of the Office of the Civil Service Commissioners.

I.9    During the period 1 January to 31 December 1998, OFTEL did not exercise any of the exceptions to fair and open competition permitted under the Recruitment Code. Excluding appointments for less than 12 months and incoming staff on loan from other government departments and agencies, OFTEL recruited 24 individuals during the period 1 January 1998 to 31 December 1998. These appointments were in the following groups:

- ◆ Senior staff (Band C and above including professional and technical)   6
- ◆ Other professional and technical staff (Band B)                       0
- ◆ Executive staff (Band B)                                             13
- ◆ Secretarial and administrative support staff (Band B and A)           5

I.10   Successful applicants by gender:

| | | |
|---|---|---|
| ◆ Senior staff | Male | 6 |
| | Female | 0 |
| ◆ Other professional and technical staff | Male | 0 |
| | Female | 0 |
| ◆ Executive staff | Male | 4 |
| | Female | 9 |
| ◆ Secretarial and administrative support staff | Male | 0 |
| | Female | 5 |

I.11   Successful applicants by ethnic origin:

| | | |
|---|---|---|
| ◆ Senior staff | White | 6 |
| ◆ Other professional and technical staff | | 0 |
| ◆ Executive staff | White | 11 |
| | Asian (Indian) | 1 |
| | Other | 1 |
| ◆ Secretarial and administrative support staff | White | 2 |
| | Black (African) | 1 |
| | Asian (Pakistani) | 1 |
| | Black (Caribbean) | 1 |

I.12   During the year, none of the successful candidates recruited through open and fair competition considered themselves disabled.

**Figure 7:** The distribution of staff across the different branches in OFTEL as at 1 December 1998 (part-time staff are shown on a full-time equivalent basis).

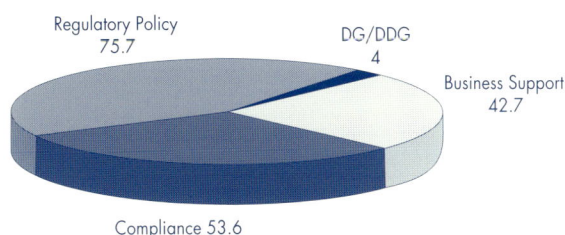

Regulatory Policy 75.7
DG/DDG 4
Business Support 42.7
Compliance 53.6

# J. **UK Standards and Approvals**

## General Approvals

J.1    General Approvals (GAs) confer approval on equipment without any need for third-party testing – it is the responsibility of manufacturers and suppliers to satisfy themselves that their products meet the GA's technical conditions. By the end of 1997, 19 GAs had been issued since 1986, although several had become redundant or obsolete.

J.2    In 1998 OFTEL began to apply GAs more widely. To prepare for the implementation of the new Terminal Equipment (RTTE) Directive, OFTEL and the DTI concluded that approval arrangements for new non-radio products should anticipate the directive's shift away from third-party testing to manufacturers' self-certification. Accordingly, where an approval route needs to be established for terminals connecting to new services, the expectation is that the approval requirements will now be covered by GAs rather than by National Technical Regulations (NTRs) or British Approvals Board for Telecommunications (BABT) Special Investigation Test Schedules (SITS).

J.3    As a result of this heightened level of activity, eleven new GAs were issued in 1998.

These were:

- GA 27 Digital decoders for connection to cable TV systems;

- GA 28 Centrex or VPN 2-wire interfaces using A.C. signalling;

- GA 29 Centrex or VPN 4-wire interfaces using A.C. signalling;

- GA 30  Centrex or VPN 2-wire interfaces using D.C. signalling on separate wires;

- GA 31  Centrex or VPN 4-wire interfaces using D.C. signalling on separate wires;

- GA 32 TETRA mobile stations approved under the TETRA MoU;

- GA 33 ATM-25 interfaces to I.432.5 or ETSI 300 811;

- GA 34 G.957 optical interfaces at STM-1/-4/-16;

- GA 35 G.703 155 Mbit/s electrical;

- GA 36 G.703 45 Mbit/s electrical;

- GA 37 SMDS High Speed Serial Interface (HSSI) to EIA/TIA 612/613.

J.4    The wider use of GAs brings advantages to customers and the industry. Because there is no third-party testing the approvals process is quicker and cheaper and products can be brought to market more rapidly. Moreover, the flexibility of the GA system means that new GAs may be issued or existing GAs varied to respond effectively to industry's needs.

## Site Specific Approvals

J.5   Site Specific Approvals (SSAs) confer section 22 approval on particular items of apparatus at specified locations in circumstances where a type approval or General Approval route is not appropriate. 111 SSAs were issued in 1998, of which all but four authorised modifications to telephones to adapt them for users with special needs. At the end of 1998, a set of generic SSAs was drafted to cover the most common cases. This is expected to result in a significant decrease in the number of individual SSAs that will need to be issued in future.

## National Technical Regulations

J.6   National Technical Regulations (NTRs) represent the minimum set of technical requirements for apparatus approval, consistent with the 'essential requirements' of the Telecommunications Terminal Equipment Directive (91/263/EEC, consolidated as 98/13/EC). NTRs apply to equipment not covered by mandatory European Common Technical Regulations (CTRs).

J.7   In 1998, there were no additions to the 15 NTRs already in force. However, preliminary work was carried out on two NTRs to apply to TETRA (Trans European Trunked Radio) terminals. Until the RTTE Directive comes into force in 2000, OFTEL General Approvals will be used to approve non-radio equipment – NTRs may be derived from their technical contents for notification and designation purposes.

## Meter Approval Scheme for Public Telecommunications Operators

J.8   The Meter Approval Scheme continued during 1998. The scheme for meter approval was introduced in May 1992 to improve customers' confidence in the accuracy of the metering and billing systems employed by Public Telecommunications Operators (PTOs). The scheme is implemented under the terms and provisions of the Telecommunications Act 1984 and may be applied to any licensed PTO or public telecommunications service provider at the discretion of the Secretary of State. PTOs within the scheme are required to submit their metering and billing systems to the BABT. Once approval has been gained, these PTOs are subject to regular audits and the approval reviewed annually.

J.9   BT first gained meter approval for its public switched telephone network in December 1994. Kingston Communications followed with approval granted in August 1996.

J.10   The eighth BABT report to the Director General on the meter approval scheme covering 1997 was published in March 1998. Following its publication, approval was further extended (by voluntary application) to the Vodafone digital mobile GSM network in March 1998 and to the Vodafone analogue mobile TACS network in July 1998.

J.11   On 30 March 1998 OFTEL published a consultation document, *Meeting customer needs for Accurate Telephone Bills.* Responses were received from all the major PTOs, service providers, advisory committees, councils, chambers of commerce and other interested parties including BABT, BSI, TMA and the DTI. A wide range of opinions was expressed, broadly indicating the following points:

- application of the scheme, though rigorous, is financially beneficial in terms of the resulting business and technical process improvements which have to be introduced by operators in order to satisfy the standards set out by the scheme.

- Consumer protection and consumer confidence would be significantly enhanced by extension of the scheme to additional PTOs and to the retail bills for mobile telephony, where these are produced by independent service providers.

- Improvements and refinements in the way the scheme is implemented could be made in the light of experience and constructive feedback from operators already in the scheme.

J.12   A revised policy on metering and billing approval is now being developed which aims to take account of these factors. Consideration is also being given to the business selection indicators and introductory phasing that should be adopted in order to extend the scheme.

## Calling Line Identity Interest Group

J.13   The Calling Line Identity (CLI) CLI Interest Group was formed in 1997 to provide a forum for informed discussion of CLI issues. Among its members are representatives from network operators and service providers, equipment manufacturers, users and consumer groups. Technical input is available from the Interconnection Standards Committee (ISC) of the Public Network Operators (PNO) interest group. The group is chaired by OFTEL.

J.14   One meeting was held in 1998. The group was involved in the preparation of a second edition of the *Code of Practice for Network Operators in relation to Customer Line Identification Display Services and Other Related Services,* published in June 1998. The Code of Practice included rules for the application of Presentation Numbers and aligned the technical terminology with that used by ETSI. The group also assisted in the production of *A Consumer's Guide to Calling Line Identification Services,* which was published electronically on the OFTEL website in June, and is intended for use by network operators to provide their customers with information about CLI services.

J.15   Other issues dealt with included the implementation of the CLI articles of the Telecoms Data Protection Directive (TDPD), 97/66/EC and the implications of Anonymous Call Rejection (ACR) and a wider use of presentation numbers.

# The Advisory Committees

## Introduction

3.1    The six Advisory Committees on Telecommunications (ACTs) represent the consumer interest in the telecommunications industry to the Director General of Telecommunications and his Office. The Committees are independent of the Director General although they are supported by his staff. (The Welsh, Scottish and Northern Irish committees also have their own local Secretaries based respectively in Cardiff, Edinburgh and Belfast.) The role of the Committees is to advise the Director General on any matter covered by his functions, whether he refers that matter to them for consideration or whether they initiate the matter in the interests of the consumer.

3.2    There are six Advisory Committees, as follows:

The country Committees;

- ◆ CCE – Consumer Communications for England, the English Advisory Committee on Telecommunications

- ◆ NIACT – Northern Ireland Advisory Committee on Telecommunications

- ◆ SACOT – Scottish Advisory Committee on Telecommunications

- ◆ WACT – Welsh Advisory Committee on Telecommunications

The special interest Committees;

- ◆ CfB – Communications for Business, the Advisory Committee on Telecommunications for Business

- ◆ DIEL – Advisory Committee on Telecommunications for Disabled and Elderly People.

3.3    The Advisory Committees are statutory bodies established by section 54 of the Telecommunications Act 1984. The members of the country Committees are appointed directly by the Secretary of State for Trade and Industry; the members of the special interest Committees are appointed by the Director General. The Committees are non-executive and purely advisory in status.

3.4    Each Committee is required to make a formal Report annually to the Director General. These Reports are published on the following pages. In addition, each Committee also publishes a leaflet on the work they have been carrying out over the last year and the activities they are undertaking for the coming year. These leaflets are available free from the Secretary to the Committee at the address given below.

3.5    The Committee Chairmen meet regularly with the Director General. Administrative support is provided by the ACT Secretariat to the Chairmen's Group, and to regular meetings of the Secretaries.

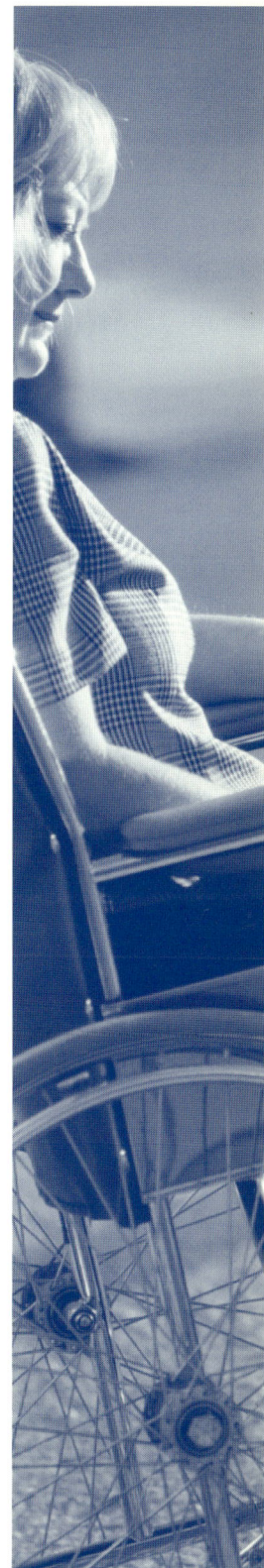

◆ **Consumer Communications for England (CCE)**
50 Ludgate Hill
London EC4M 7JJ
Tel: 0171-634 5301 (voice)
Tel: 0171-634 8769 (Minicom)
e-mail: cce@acts.org.uk

◆ **Communications for Business (CfB)**
50 Ludgate Hill
London EC4M 7JJ
Tel: 0171-634 5301 (voice)
Tel: 0171-634 8769 (Minicom)
e-mail: cfb@acts.org.uk

◆ **Advisory Committee on Telecommunications for Disabled and Elderly People (DIEL)**
50 Ludgate Hill
London EC4M 7JJ
Tel: 0171-634 5301 (voice)
Tel: 0171-634 8769 (Minicom)
e-mail: diel@acts.org.uk

◆ **Northern Ireland Advisory Committee on Telecommunications (NIACT)**
7th Floor
Chamber of Commerce House
22 Great Victoria Street
Belfast
BT2 7QA
Tel: 01232 244113
e-mail: niact@acts.org.uk

◆ **Scottish Advisory Committee on Telecommunications (SACOT)**
2 Greenside Lane
Edinburgh EH1 3AH
Tel: 0131 244 5576
e-mail: sacot@acts.org.uk

◆ **Welsh Advisory Committee on Telecommunications (WACT)**
Caradog House
St Andrews Place
Cardiff CF1 3BE
Tel: 01222 374028
e-mail: wact@acts.org.uk

Consumer complaints and enquiries should be made by phone on **0845 714 5000**

The ACTs have their own Internet site at www.acts.org.uk

# Report of Consumer Communications for England (CCE)

## Membership and activity in 1998

3.6    Four new members were appointed to CCE during the year following the recruitment procedure set up by the DTI. Following a competitive selection process, in which the Chairman took an active part, members with a range of consumer protection experience were appointed. These appointments brought the committee up to full strength and add welcome knowledge and experience to the existing expertise on the committee. Three members left the committee during the year. Two came to the end of their periods of appointment and one member moved to live abroad. A membership list follows this report.

3.7    The committee held its normal quarterly meetings and supplemented these by working in sub-groups on particular issues. In July CCE agreed to open future meetings to the public. *Ad hoc* sub-groups met to discuss issues such as the European Commission Green Paper on convergence and to plan a seminar on utility regulation review. The Chairman attended all three of the Advisory Committee Chairmen's meetings with the Director General. The Chairman joined the Chairmen of the other Advisory Committees on Telecommunications (ACTs) and met with the Minister for Competition and Consumer Affairs at the DTI.

3.8    OFTEL staff gave presentations to Committee members on various subjects including carrier preselection, payphone regulation, implementation of the revised Voice Telephony Directive, PRS services and plans for a review of universal service. This input is very welcome and usefully informed debate at CCE meetings. Regular attendance by a representative of OFTEL's Consumer Representations section meant that the committee was kept informed on changing patterns of consumer complaints received by OFTEL over the year. Committee members also attended a presentation by BT on convergence and a member visited the BT laboratories at Martlesham Heath. In July members attended a seminar on Utility Review organised by the Centre for Regulated Industries and Consumers' Association.

3.9    The Chairman participated in the work of the Director General's Consumer Panel on the convergence of the telecommunications and broadcasting industries. Members of the committee took part in initiatives organised by OFTEL, including the Price Comparison Working Party and the Small Business Task Force. CCE has also been represented at the Telecommunications Directory Information Code of Practice Working Group organised by the Data Protection Registrar. Members have also attended OFTEL training courses where appropriate.

3.10   The ACTs' Internet site went live in May and CCE has its own section. Agendas and minutes of meetings, CCE responses to OFTEL consultation documents and other useful information about the work of the Committee are available. CCE was represented on the ACTs stand at the Institute of Trading Standards Administration (ITSA) annual conference, where useful contacts were made.

## Major areas of work

3.11 At the beginning of the year CCE was represented alongside the other country ACTs at a Joint Hearing held by the Monopolies and Mergers Commission (MMC) as part of its work on the reference made to it by the Director General on calls to mobiles. CCE also made a written submission to the MMC.

3.12 CCE hosted a seminar in April to discuss the Utility Review Green Paper which was well attended by a number of consumer bodies and organisations with an interest in telecommunications. The Chairman hosted the event and encouraged debate on the issues from the floor. The proposals likely to have an impact on telecommunications consumers, such as the setting up of a Telecommunications Consumer Council, were the focus of discussion.

3.13 During the year CCE contributed responses to a number of OFTEL consultations, including *A Better Deal for Payphone Users and Meeting Customer Needs for Accurate Telephone Bills*. The committee also contributed to and took an interest in consultations initiated elsewhere. Responses were made to DTI consultations, including implementation of Directive 97/66/EC on the *Processing of Data and the Protection of Privacy in the Telecommunications Sector, A Fair Deal for Consumers – Modernising the Framework for Utility Regulation and Utility Consumer Councils*. CCE also responded to the European Commission Green Paper on the Convergence of Telecommunications, Media and Information Technology Sectors, and the Implications for Regulation.

3.14 The Committee produced its own annual report leaflet which itemises the work carried out in the past year and its plans for 1999. This is available from the secretariat.

# Committee Membership

*Chairman*

**Moira Black CBE**
Chairman, Riverside Community Healthcare NHS Trust. London.

*Members*

**Sue Bloomfield** (to July 1998)
Consultant, previously worked for Consumers' Association. London.

**Ian Bryce** (to July 1998)
Retired Accountant. Bridlington.

**Peter Collins** (from October 1998)
Non Executive Chairman of a software company. Lancashire.

**Robert Little**
Former Director, telecommunications equipment manufacturing. Nottingham.

**Brian Love**
Consultant specialising in business telecommunications. Warwick.

**Barbara McClennan**
Lecturer in Media, Darlington College of Technology. Sunderland.

**Brian McNally**
Retired Chief Trading Standards Officer. Norfolk.

**Claire Milne** (to July 1998)
Consultant specialising in social aspects of telecommunications, previously
worked for BT. Essex.

**Siva Lingham Moodley** (from October 1998)
Director of Childline Headquarters Counselling Services. London.

**John O'Reilly**
Professor of Telecommunications, University College, London.

**Peter Sayers**
Managing Director of IT company. Cheltenham.

**Philippa Thompson** (from October 1998)
Director of Consumer Congress. West Sussex.

**Joyce Wood**
US regulatory lawyer and telecommunications consultant. East Sussex.

**James Woodward-Nutt** (from October 1998)
Retired broadcasting engineer, Vice President of the National Federation of
Consumer Groups. Surrey.

# Report of the Northern Ireland Advisory Committee on Telecommunications (NIACT)

## Membership and activity in 1998

3.15  NIACT members are appointed across a wide geographical spread and covering a great depth of consumer interest. 1998 saw the resignation of a valuable member, Dr Jim Shields, who made a great contribution with his experience in technical matters. Mr Moore Kennedy was appointed to the Committee with a background in customer service and complaint handling with one of the major telecommunications operators.

3.16  The Committee held four meetings during the year. At the final quarterly meeting, NIACT had the opportunity to meet OFTEL's Director General, and the Director of the Office of Telecommunications Regulation for the Republic of Ireland, Etain Doyle. This meeting was also attended by representatives of the major telecommunications operators.

3.17  NIACT hosted its Annual Conference in March – Telecom '98 Consumer Choice (and What You Need to Know) – with key speakers from OFTEL and the General Consumer Council for Northern Ireland.

3.18  The Committee continued to keep in close contact with Government Departments and the telephone companies operating in Northern Ireland.

3.19  Regular liaison took place with OFTEL and with the other Advisory Committees on Telecommunications. The Chairman, members or Secretary attended OFTEL working groups covering topics such as Carrier Preselection and mobile phones. NIACT was represented on the National Code and Number Change Working Group, and at Telecommunications Advisory Committee (TAC) meetings and various other events locally and in Great Britain. NIACT members joined other consumer groups on a successful one-day training workshop on 'How to be a Consumer Representative' organised by the General Consumer Council for Northern Ireland.

3.20  NIACT continued to work with the network of local Northern Ireland TACs. These reflect the perceptions of local telephone users in their areas and have contributed in the past year to discussions within the Committee on subjects such as numbering policy, pricing and the role of consumer representation.

## Work of the Committee

3.21  In March the Committee organised a conference that explored Telecommunications and Consumer Choice. Speakers included representatives from the mobile, cable and Internet sectors. The conference informed consumers on developments in the telecommunications industry to empower them.

3.22 One of the key issues to which NIACT made significant input was the proposed changes to numbering in Northern Ireland which will take place in April 2000. NIACT members also attended a meeting in Dublin with Etain Doyle, the Director of the Office of Telecommunications Regulation. The main items under discussion included numbering patterns in the Republic of Ireland and effective use of telecommunications to improve trade with Northern Ireland. The Committee was also given an update on how Ireland is meeting its directives such as free trade in telecommunications.

3.23 NIACT continued to press BT to introduce a local call rate throughout Northern Ireland.

The Committee made responses to the following consultation documents during the year:

- ◆ *Telecommunications Services for People with Disabilities;*
- ◆ *A Better Deal for Payphone Users;*
- ◆ *Improving Accountability;*
- ◆ *Beyond the Telephone, the Television and the PC – Regulation of the Electronic Communications Industry;*
- ◆ *Prices of Calls to Mobile Phones;*
- ◆ *Developing Number Administration;*
- ◆ *Proposal to Determine that BT has Interface Control in the Supply of Certain Telecommunications Services.*

3.24 On behalf of NIACT, the Chairman submitted a response to Dr Kim Howells, the Minister for Consumer Affairs and Competition on the consultation document on Utility Consumer Councils.

3.25 NIACT is concerned that Northern Ireland consumers are actively represented at a regional level in the new representative structures. It is vital that there remains a Northern Ireland consumer body that will handle consumer complaints and a wide range of consumer concerns at local level. The setting up of the Northern Ireland Assembly again emphasises the need for a regional telecommunications consumer body.

## Complaints and Representations

3.26 The volume of complaints received by the Committee's Secretariat increased during the year, and in the last quarter there was a dramatic increase in the number of complaints relating to one mobile operator and with the market entry of various re-sellers. Increasing awareness of the role of NIACT partly accounted for this increase in the number of complaints.

**Table 9:** Summary of complaints and enquiries received by NIACT during 1998

| Category of Complaint | 1997 | 1998 |
|---|---|---|
| Disputed accounts | 120 | 28 |
| Billing matters | 41 | 32 |
| Fault repair service | 6 | 8 |
| Provision of service | 13 | 18 |
| Payphones | 7 | 6 |
| Operator services | 0 | 3 |
| Quality of service | 15 | 102 |
| Compensation scheme | 4 | 4 |
| Telephone books | 27 | 8 |
| Customer confidentiality | 5 | 30 |
| Uninvited calls | 2 | 3 |
| Arbitration | 1 | 0 |
| Price changes | 15 | 9 |
| Charges | 17 | 36 |
| Deposits | 3 | 1 |
| Unsolicited faxes | 0 | 30 |
| Miscellaneous | 102 | 51 |
| Re-sellers contracts | 0 | 82 |
| **Totals** | **378** | **451** |

# Committee Membership

*Chairman*

**JLC Thompson BA BBS DL**
Company Director, President Royal Ulster Agricultural Society.

*Members*

**Miss Claire Aiken**
Managing Director, public relations consultancy. Belfast

**Mr John Campbell**
Executive Consultant. Lisburn

**Mr Brian St. J. Collins**
Lecturer in Business and Consumer Law, University of Ulster, Magee College.
Londonderry

**Mrs Celine Corrigan**
Chartered accountant and registered auditor. Antrim

**Mr Moore Kennedy**
Tourism Consultant for the Northern Ireland Growth Challenge. Belfast

**Mr Alan Kerr**
Communications Manager, Royal Group of Hospitals and Dental Hospital and
Social Services Trust. Belfast

**Mr John Kerr BSc**
Chairman of European Funded Cross Border Committee providing use of
telephony in rural areas. Londonderry

**Mr Ian McPherson**
Retired IT Executive with the Northern Bank. Belfast

**Ms Jean McVitty**
Councillor with Fermanagh District Council. Enniskillen

**Mr Seamus Magee**
Chief Officer, Southern Health and Social Services Council. Belfast

*Secretary*
**Mr John A Stringer**

*Assistant Secretary*
**Miss Catherine McQuitty**

# Report of the Scottish Advisory Committee On Telecommunications (SACOT)

## Membership and activity during 1998

3.27 One new member of the Committee was appointed, three including the outgoing Chairman retired, and two members resigned. The Committee held four meetings during the year, some of which were attended by senior representatives of network operators in Scotland, with which the Committee endeavours to maintain close links, and by senior officials from OFTEL. All meetings of the Committee were held at the Secretary's office in Edinburgh.

3.28 The Chairman participated in discussions with the Director General and the other Advisory Committee Chairmen, as well as attending seminars and workshops on particular topics of interest.

## Major areas of work

3.29 During the year under report SACOT:

- Responded to the Department of Trade and Industry Consultative Document *A Fair Deal For Consumers: Modernising The Framework For Utility Regulation,* and also submitted comments on the subsequent phase of the consultative process concerning the establishment of statutory Consumer Councils. While giving general support to the proposals for improved representation of consumers' interests, SACOT emphasised the need to ensure that there was an effective structure for the representation of users of telecommunications services in Scotland, preferably on a statutory basis.

- Submitted views to the Director General and participated in discussions on a wide range of OFTEL consultative documents and other initiatives, including:

  - *A Better Deal for Payphone Users: OFTEL's Proposals for Payphone Regulation in the UK;*

  - *Freephone Numbers: Options for the Future;*

  - *Developing Number Administration;*

  - *Improving Accountability: Further Steps;*

  - *Proposals for Publishing Information on Complaints Received by OFTEL;*

- *A Review of Telecommunication Licence Fees in the UK;*

- *OFTEL's Work Programme 1998/99;*

- *OFTEL Mobile Phone Working Group;*

- *Carrier Preselection;*

- *OFTEL Statement on the Principles of Affordability.*

◆ Reviewed the committee's strategic framework and identified a number of priorities and key objectives for action in 1999. These include:

  - ensuring that the proposed Telecommunications Consumer Council has sufficient powers and resources to do its job properly;

  - improving SACOT's own effectiveness in handling complaints and making SACOT's work better known;

  - contributing to the forthcoming review of European Union telecommunications legislation.

◆ Using the services of an external consultant, explored further the manner in which the Committee's profile might usefully be enhanced, and considered ways of making SACOT more accessible to consumers (with particular reference to the publication of dates of Committee meetings, agendas and papers, minutes on SACOT's section of the ACT website).

◆ Maintained contact with existing public telecommunications operators (PTOs) in Scotland through a series of meetings with senior managers to discuss issues of mutual interest.

◆ Commissioned a research study into consumers' perceptions of choice of telecommunications operator and of tariff, and into consumers' experience of getting telecommunications problems resolved.

## Complaints and Representations

3.30 A summary of complaints received during the year under report in respect of telecommunications service in Scotland is given below.

**Table 10:** Summary of complaints and enquiries received by SACOT during 1998

| Category of complaint | 1997 | 1998 |
|---|---|---|
| Disputed accounts | 296 | 93 |
| Billing matters (other) | 917 | 646 |
| Fault repair service | 184 | 127 |
| Provision of service | 439 | 333 |
| Payphones | 27 | 16 |
| Operator services | 12 | 163 |
| Quality of service | 52 | 26 |
| Compensation scheme | 40 | 10 |
| Telephone books | 39 | 19 |
| Customer confidentiality | 43 | 25 |
| Uninvited calls | 175 | 341 |
| Arbitration | 23 | 1 |
| Price changes | 14 | 1 |
| Charges | 266 | 185 |
| Deposits | 3 | 0 |
| Miscellaneous | 624 | 336 |
| **Totals** | **3154** | **2322** |

3.31 It has been possible to provide a comparison between this year's complaints and those for last year only up to the end of September. The reason for this is that the way in which SACOT measures and records complaint activity changed from 1 October 1998, in order to make the information gathered in this connection more meaningful. The computer database which has been developed to accommodate this change is still being refined. Therefore, at the time of this report's preparation (January 1999) it is not possible to provide anything other than a very broad picture of complaint activity in the last three months of 1998. For example in the three month period from October to December SACOT dealt with a total of 701 complaints and enquiries, covering 894 separate issues, focusing in the main on billing matters, quality of customer service and unsolicited faxes. Fuller details will be given in next year's annual report.

# Committee Membership

*Chairman*

**Jeremy Mitchell** (from November 1998)
Consumer policy adviser and Public Interest Board
Member of the Personal Investment Authority. Edinburgh.

**W K Begg OBE** (to September 1998)
Chairman, Engineering Group. Glasgow.

*Members*

**D A Gardner**
Director and broadcaster, commercial radio. Inverness.

**C J Griffith**
Business development manager. Dumfries/Cumbria.

**M Hagger**
Management consultant. Aberdeenshire.

**N M Hope** (to September 1998)
Retired telecommunications engineer. Aberdeen.

**Mrs C J Jones BSc ARSM** (to September 1998)
Oil exploration geoscientist. Lockerbie.

**K Murray**
Director, textile manufacturer. Isle of Lewis.

**Mrs W D Reynolds**
Dietician. Argyll.

**Alistair Robertson** (from November 1998)
Retired IT strategy manager.

**Mrs C B Watkin** (to March 1998)
Education adviser. Arbroath.

**Mr B T Stevens**
Retired airport administrator. Shetland.

**Professor H Williams** (to December 1998)
Professor of Management Science, University of Strathclyde, Glasgow.

**P Wilson**
Former Councillor and Convenor of Lothian Regional Council. Edinburgh.

*Secretary*
**R L L King**

# Report of the Welsh Advisory Committee on Telecommunications (WACT)

## Membership and activity during 1998

3.32  Five new members were appointed in November 1998 to fill vacancies on the Committee. Two existing members were re-appointed for a further term.

3.33  The Committee met on four occasions during the year, twice in Cardiff, once in Aberystwyth and once in Machynlleth.

3.34  Through its members and secretariat the Committee kept in touch with TACs throughout Wales. WACT also continued to maintain close contacts with the public network operators active in Wales and the Government Departments.

3.35  Regular liaison took place with OFTEL and the other Advisory Committees through attendance at meetings by the Chairman, members and the secretariat, which was strengthened by the addition of a deputy secretary to help cope with the additional work of Grant in Aid.

## Major areas of work

3.36  Key topics considered by the Committee during the year include:

- *Market Research for Telecommunications of Rural and Urban Users in Wales;*
- *Availability of Advanced Services in Wales* (eg calling line identification and ISDN2 & 2e);
- *North Wales Franchise* (Metrocable – to cover North Wales down to Dolgellau and to use microwave for the last link to the home using MVDS short range. This will be rolled out over five years.);
- *A Better Deal for Telephone Users;*
- *A Fair Deal for Consumers;*
- *Regulating Communications;*
- *Freephone Numbers: Options for the Future;*
- *Developing Number Administration;*
- *Privacy in Telecommunications.*

## Complaints and representations

3.37  A summary of complaints and enquiries received during the year under the report is shown in the table opposite.

**Table 11:** Summary of complaints and enquiries received by WACT during 1998

| Category of Complaint | 1996 | 1997 | 1998* |
|---|---|---|---|
| Disputed Accounts | 43 | 23 | 63 |
| Billing Matters | 263 | 293 | 153 |
| Fault Repair Service | 179 | 228 | 108 |
| Provision of Service | 106 | 109 | 97 |
| Payphones | 9 | 0 | 7 |
| Operator services | 9 | 0 | 2 |
| Quality of service | 31 | 29 | 5 |
| Compensation scheme | 42 | 17 | 6 |
| Telephone books | 23 | 13 | 6 |
| Customer confidentiality | 0 | 12 | 1 |
| Uninvited calls | 14 | 41 | 117 |
| Arbitration | 1 | 0 | 0 |
| Price changes | 13 | 49 | 3 |
| Charges | 42 | 39 | 32 |
| Mobile phones | 0 | 72 | 128 |
| Miscellaneous | 188 | 301 | 152 |
| **Totals** | **963** | **1235** | **880** |

*Note: It has only been possible to provide comparative figures up until September 1998. Since October 1998 the way in which complaints data is recorded has been changed in order to make the data more meaningful. As the new system is still being developed as this report is being written (January 1999) it is only possible to provide a broad picture of complaint data in the later three months of 1998. In the three months to December 1998, WACT dealt with a total of 407 complaints and enquiries; these were mainly concerned with billing matters, quality of customer service and repairs.

# Committee Membership

*Chairman*

**Professor M D Tedd MA Ceng MBCS**
Professor of Computer Science, University of Wales, Aberystwyth.

*Members*

**Mrs P J Blackwell**
Member of Brecon and Radnorshire Community Health Council. Builth Wells

**Mrs K M Counsell** (from November 1998)
Senior Lecturer in Law, University of Glamorgan. Pendoylan

**Mr D R Dutton** (to September 1998)
Retired businessman. Wrexham

**Mr R J Edwards** (from November 1998)
Head of Public Affairs, NSPCC Wales/Midlands. Prestatyn

**Mr D O Evans**
Businessman. Anglesey

**Mrs D Hammett** (to May 1998)
Teacher. Swansea

**Mr I A Lebbon-Corwen** (from November 1998)
Local Government Officer. Mold

**Mr J Maynard BSc MBCS** (to September 1998)
Managing Director. Lusis

**Mr J R Simmonds** (from November 1998)
Local Government Officer. Llandrindod Wells

**Ms L Tomos**
Librarian Service, Director Wales Information Network. Dolgellau.

**Mr W Ward** (from November 1998)
Part-time lecturer in IT and computer consultant. Prestatyn

**Miss G Williams**
Retired accountant. Newport

*Secretary*
**G J Mackenzie**

# Report of Communications for Business Committee (CfB)

## Activity during the year

3.38 Communications for Business was previously known as BACT – the Business Advisory Committee on Telecommunications. The Chairman felt that the change of name would reflect the Committee's interest in the widening range of electronic communications technologies and services available to businesses over telecommunications networks.

3.39 Early in the year, OFTEL established a task force to investigate the telecommunications needs of the SME sector, the reasons for poor take-up of telecommunications services, and the options for action by the industry, business support services, government, OFTEL, and others to promote use by SMEs of information and communications technologies. The Chairman of CfB is a member of this task force.

3.40 When the task force was set up the Chairman agreed that, as CfB had not reached clear conclusions regarding its role and agenda for the coming year, OFTEL resources should be switched to support the task force for 1998. It was hoped that the task force project would deliver answers to the issues noted above and in doing so might also identify ways in which the small business sector could most effectively advise OFTEL of its needs and input to OFTEL consultations and thus provide some new impetus to CfB. The conclusion of the task force's work is expected during 1999.

3.41 During 1998 therefore, the Communications for Business committee did not meet. The Chairman participated in the SME task force, and continued to attend regular meetings of the Advisory Committee Chairmen with the Director General. Other CfB members participated in ad hoc meetings with members of the other Advisory Committees.

3.42 The Committee did however respond to a number of OFTEL consultation papers:

- *Draft terms of reference for the SME task force;*
- *Consultation on telecommunications licence fees in the UK;*
- *Proposals for publishing information on complaints received by OFTEL.*

The Committee responded to DTI consultations:

- *A Fair Deal for Consumers – Modernising the Framework for Utility Regulation;*
- *Consultation on Utility Consumer Councils.*

## Membership

3.43  The terms of office of two long-standing members came to an end in April. Richard Furey had been an active member of the committee since 1987 and Margaret Seymour since 1992. In addition Dawn Penso's first term of office ended in May, and Oliver Makower resigned in July.

3.44  At the end of the year, CfB had three members: Peter Calver, Spencer Wrench, and Robin Kemp. Membership will be a matter for consideration by the Chairman and Director General during 1999.

# Committee Membership

*Chairman*

**Peter Calver**
Managing Director, sports simulation software. London. Term of office:
August 1996-September 1999

*Members*

**Richard Furey**
Managing Director, electronic systems design. County Antrim
Term of office: April 1987-April 1998.

**Robin Kemp**
Former Managing Director, flooring ceiling and insulation products. Berkshire
Term of office: December 1996-December 1999.

**Oliver Makower**
Former Chairman, textile business. Oxfordshire
Term of office: September 1996 to resignation in July 1998.

**Dawn Penso**
Partner, training and employment consultancy. London
Term of office: May 1995-May 1998.

**Margaret Seymour**
Managing Director, swimming pool design and construction. Lanarkshire
Term of office: April 1992-April 1998.

**Spencer Wrench**
Managing Director, greetings cards, car retail, cable consultation and installation. Cambridgeshire
Term of office: December 1996-November 1999.

# Report of the Advisory Committee On Telecommunications for Disabled and Elderly People (DIEL)

## Promoting telephone access for disabled and elderly people

3.45 DIEL continued to pursue a goal of inclusiveness. The Committee believes that telecommunications services and equipment should be 'designed for all' and available in ways that do not exclude elderly and disabled consumers. This approach relies on the positive actions of telecommunications companies, be they network operators, service providers or equipment manufacturers, and their recognition of the sizeable market opportunity represented by elderly and disabled telecommunications consumers. The approach also relies on OFTEL's continued ability to enforce licence obligations and to champion the additional needs of disabled and elderly people in relation to telecommunications.

## Apparatus

3.46 During the early and latter parts of 1998, OFTEL issued first a consultation document and then a statement on *Telecommunications Services for Disabled and Elderly People.* DIEL assisted and advised OFTEL when it prepared the consultation document, although all the views in the document did not reflect those of DIEL. DIEL made its own views known by responding fully to both OFTEL publications. In particular DIEL was, and continues to be, concerned about the importance of apparatus.

3.47 The Committee believes that equal access cannot be achieved without reference to apparatus. Lack of suitable equipment remains a barrier to access to even basic telephony for many disabled people. OFTEL's statement contained specific proposals to the DTI on the modification of the licences of most telecommunications operators by the inclusion of a specific licence condition in relation to disabled consumers. However, OFTEL's draft licence condition did not take up the issue of equipment on the basis that the Telecommunications Act 1984 does not authorise OFTEL to impose obligations on operators in relation to the supply of apparatus. DIEL strongly argued to both OFTEL and the DTI that the issue of apparatus is key to meeting the needs of elderly and disabled people. In 1999 DIEL will continue to press this case with DTI.

## Other consultations

3.48 DIEL responded to a number of OFTEL statements and consultations, including those on *Provision of Directory Information and A Better Deal for Payphone Users.* DIEL took a keen interest in the Government's proposals for utility regulation and responded to the DTI's public consultation paper on

Consumer Councils, firmly arguing the need for at least one member of a future Telecommunications Consumer Council to have personal experience of issues affecting elderly and disabled consumers. The Committee also responded to the Department for Education and Employment's White Paper on the role and functions of a Disability Rights Commission.

## Working with others

3.49 DIEL continued to strengthen ties with other bodies. DIEL organised and hosted a workshop on 'Telecoms for Elderly People' and a seminar on 'Information Provision for Disabled and Elderly People about Telecommunications'. Both events were well attended by representatives from a number of organisations that work to promote the interests of elderly and disabled people, from consumer bodies, Government Departments and telecommunications companies.

3.50 Early in 1998 the Chairman accompanied the other ACT Chairmen and met with the Minister for Competition and Consumer Affairs at the DTI. DIEL was encouraged that the then Minister took a genuine interest in the needs of elderly and disabled consumers. The Chairman ensured that DIEL's views were represented as a member of OFTEL's Broadcasting and Convergence Consumer Panel.

3.51 In order to raise awareness amongst OFTEL staff, a Disability Awareness Seminar was held in March. DIEL hopes that such an event will be repeated and become a part of core training for all OFTEL staff.

3.52 DIEL maintained regular contact with outside consumer bodies with similar interests. These included the Telecommunications Action Group (TAG) for deaf and speech-impaired people, the UK Cost 219 Group which monitors developments affecting disabled end elderly telecommunications users as part of a wider European project and the Working Group for the Hearing Impaired (WGHI).

3.53 Three new members were appointed to the Committee and three retired during the year when their period of appointment came to an end. At the end of the year there was one vacancy unfilled. The Committee met on four occasions, and meetings sometimes included presentations and discussions involving representatives from OFTEL, BT and other organisations. The Chairman, several members and the Secretariat represented DIEL on other occasions, including meetings with the DTI, the Department of Health to discuss the problem of mobile telephones interfering with hearing aids and at a seminar to discuss the Utilities Review.

# Committee Membership

*Chairman*

**Jean Gaffin OBE**
Former Executive Director, National Council for Hospice and Specialist Palliative Care Services. Middlesex.

*Members*

**John Barnes**
Chartered telecommunications engineer. Essex.

**Robin Birch CB**
Vice President, Age Concern England. Oxford.

**David Dunsmuir** (to February 1998)
Former Director, Disability Scotland.

**Pauline Hermann** (from March 1998)
Project Manager for Continuing Care Services. London.

**Caroline Jacobs**
Development Manager, Research Institute for Consumer Affairs. London.

**David Mann**
Campaigns Officer RNIB. Co. Antrim.

**Michael Martin OBE** (to February 1998)
Consultant in the speech and hearing field. West Sussex.

**Brain McGinnis**
Special Adviser, Mencap. London.

**Shcila Porter** (to May 1998)
Formerly Principal Social Services Officer, Neath Port Talbot County Borough Council.

**Stephen Smith** (from March 1998)
Technical Advisor to the Association of Social and Community Alarms Providers. Hampshire.

**Ross Trotter**
Secretary, Telecommunications Action Group (for deaf, deafened, hard of hearing and deaf-blind people). West Yorkshire.

**Bob Twitchin**
Consultant in the fields of disability and information and communications technology. Middlesex.

**Sue Williams** (from August 1998)
Nurse Adviser to the Greater Glasgow Health Board. Ayrshire.

# Advisory Body On Fair Trading In Telecommunications – Annual Report 1998

3.54  The Advisory Body on Fair Trading in Telecommunications was established in December 1996 to advise the Director General on enforcement of the Fair Trading Condition (incorporated as Condition 18A in BT's Telecommunications Act Licence and subsequently incorporated into 250 other operators' licences). Under the Fair Trading Condition, either the Director General or the Licensee can ask for a matter to be considered by the Advisory Body before the making of a Final Determination.

## Membership during 1998

3.55  The ABFTT is an independent body currently comprising five members from a variety of backgrounds. The Chairman is Jeremy Lever QC. During the year Dr Mark Armstrong and Professor Geoffrey Whittington ceased to be members and Professor Michael Utton was appointed a new member. At the end of 1998 membership was as follows:

## Activity during 1998

3.56  During the year the ABFTT discussed with OFTEL various aspects of its procedures; as a result a number of changes were agreed. In particular, in order to facilitate the ABFTT's examination of the issues raised in any specific reference within the tight timetable set by the relevant licence conditions, a Statement of Facts is to be issued by the Director General, around the time a reference is made, both to the Licensee concerned and to the complainant to enable them to comment. The Statement of Facts and any comments are then to be passed to the ABFTT. In addition, at the time any specific matter is referred to the ABFTT the Director General is to appoint a Case Secretary – who is not to have had any direct involvement in the matter – to the ABFTT. The draft for amending the Procedural Notes of the ABFTT also involve a number of other, mostly administrative, changes; they are due to go out for consultation early in 1999.

# Committee Membership

*Chairman*

**Jeremy Lever QC**
Senior Dean, All Souls College, Oxford.

*Members*

**Hans Liesner**
Former Deputy Chairman, Monopolies and Mergers Commission.

**Martin Howe**
Former Director of the Competition Policy Division, Office of Fair Trading.

**Teresa Smallbone**
Consultant to the National Consumer Council and Senior Lecturer in Marketing,
Oxford Brookes University.

**Michael Utton**
Professor of Economics, University of Reading.

# List of publications during 1998

## ABOUT OFTEL

OFTEL Management Plan 1998-99 Projects, Programmes and their Managers – OFTEL reorganisation (11/98)

OFTEL's Draft Work programme for 1998/99 and beyond – (3/98)

OFTEL's Draft Work programme for 1998/99 and beyond – Summary Guide (3/98)

Improving Accountability: further steps – Statement (2/98)

Consulting on OFTEL's work programme 1998/99 (2/98)

OFTEL's Annual Report for 1997 (3/98)

## BROADCASTING

OFTEL's response to the European Commission's working document summarising the results of the public consultation on the Green paper on the Convergence of the Telecommunications, Media and Information Technology sectors. – Response (11/98)

Digital television and interactive services: ensuring access on fair, reasonable and non-discriminatory terms – Consultative Document (3/98)

Beyond the telephone, the television and the PC – Regulation of the electronic communications industry – (3/98)

Conditional Access Charges for Digital Television – Statement (2/98)

Beyond The Telephone, The Television and The PC – II – OFTEL's first submission to the Culture Media and Sports Select Committee Inquiry into audio-visual communications and the regulation of broadcasting (1/98)

## COMPETITION

Access to bandwidth: Bringing higher bandwidth services to the consumer – Consultative Document (12/98)

Recovering the Costs of Carrier Pre-Selection – Statement (11/98)

Review of Cable and Wireless Communications' status as a Well Established Operator – Consultative Document (10/98)

Operators with Significant Market Power for the application of detailed rules under purposes of the EC Voice Telephony and Universal Service Directive (10/98)

Carrier Pre-Selection in the UK – (7/98)

Interconnection & Interoperability of Services over Telephony Networks – Statement (4/98)

Identification of operators with Significant Market power for the Application of Detailed Rules under Purposes of the EC Voice Telephony and Universal Service Directive – Consultative Document (4/98)

Rights and obligations to interconnect under the EU Interconnection directive – Consultative Document (3/98)

Continued

Identification of Significant Market Power for the purposes of the Leased Lines Directive (as amended) (3/98)

Delivering the benefits of the information age to customers in Hull – Consultative Document (3/98)

Identification of Significant Market Power for the purposes of the Interconnection Directive – Statement (2/98)

Effective Competition Review – Statement (2/98)

## CONSUMER ISSUES

Proposals for Publishing Information on Complaints Received by OFTEL – Consultation Document (11/98)

Comparable Performance Indicators (11/98)

Telecommunications services for people with disabilities – Consumer Guide (9/98)

Telecommunications services for people with disabilities – Statement (9/98)

Your directory information: changes to give consumers more choice – Consumer Guide (9/98)

Provision of Directory Information Services and Products – Statement (9/98)

Premium Rate Services – Letter to Chief Executives (8/98)

Comparable Performance Indicators (5/98)

Towards Better Telecommunications for Customers, 1997/8 progress report – Market Research report (3/98)

Meeting consumer needs for accurate telephone bills – Consultative Document (3/98)

Telecommunications Services for people with disabilities – Consumer Guide (2/98)

Telecommunications Services for people with disabilities – Consultative Document (2/98)

A Better Deal for Payphone Users – Consumer booklet (2/98)

A Better Deal for Payphone Users – Consultative Document (2/98)

Improving Accountability: further steps – Statement (2/98)

## FAIR TRADING

Interconnection & Interoperability of Services over Telephony Networks – Statement (4/98)

Personal numbering services – Consultative Document (3/98)

Guidelines on Wiring – Guidelines (2/98)

Continued

## INFORMATION AND FEEDBACK

Table of international accounting rates – (12/98)

Table of international accounting rates – (9/98)

Table of international accounting rates – (7/98)

The collection and publication of international call information – (7/98)

Advanced telecommunications services: awareness, take up and availability in the UK – a NERA report (7/98)

Regulatory issues associated with multi-utilities – Joint paper by Utility Regulators (5/98)

Comparable Performance Indicators (5/98)

## LICENSING

A Review of Telecommunication Licence Fees in the UK – Consultative Document (11/98)

Statement on the principles of affordability – Statement (11/98)

Review of Cable and Wireless Communications' status as a Well Established Operator – Consultative Document (10/98)

OFTEL Statement on the Review of the Telecommunications Act Licence of Kingston Communications (Hull) plc and Kingston upon Hull City Council – Statement (7/98)

Modification of the Licences of Orange and Mercury Personal Communications (MPCL) – Statement (4/98)

Delivering the benefits of the information age to customers in Hull – Consultative Document (3/98)

## NUMBERING

Number Portability – Functional Specification – published by OFTEL's non-geographic number portability focus group (10/98)

Developing Number Administration – Consultation Document (7/98)

Freephone numbers: Options for the future – (7/98)

National Code and Number Change Framework Document – (5/98)

Non-geographic Number Portability costs and charges – Determination and explanatory document (3/98)

Northern Ireland: new telephone prefixes Easter 2000 – Numbering Briefing (1/98)

## PRICING AND PRICE CONTROL

British Telecommunications plc – A report on a reference under section 13 of the Telecommunications Act 1984 on the charges made by British Telecommunications plc for calls from its subscribers to phones connected to the networks of Cellnet and Vodafone – MMC (12/98)

Cellnet and Vodafone – Reports on references under section 13 of the Telecommunications Act 1984 on the charges made by Cellnet and Vodafone for terminating calls from fixed-line networks – MMC (12/98)

Determination under Condition 13.40 of BT's Licence to disapply Condition 13.35 of BT's Licence with regard to the interconnect charge for conveying traffic at the daytime rate between Northern Ireland and the Republic of Ireland – Determination and Explanatory Document (11/98)

Statement on the principles of affordability – Statement (11/98)

Tariffing Issues: Bundling of Inbound and Outbound Services – Statement (10/98)

Consultation on removing the obligation on CWC to publish backhaul prices – Letter of consultation (10/98)

Determination of the Payphone Access Charge – Determination (8/98)

Determination of competitiveness of access to indirect access operator services from payphones – Determination (8/98)

OFTEL's submission to the Monopolies and Mergers Commission inquiry into the prices of calls to mobile phones – (5/98)

Interconnection & Interoperability of Services over Telephony Networks – Statement (4/98)

Determination of Final Charges for BT's standard services for year ending 31 March 1997 – Determination (4/98)

Prices of calls to mobile phones – Statement (3/98)

## TECHNICAL

Voluntary code of practice on call answering and charging arising from the attachment of private equipment and systems to the public switched telephone network – Code of Practice (NICC) (10/98)

Proposal to determine that BT has Interface Control in the supply of certain telecommunications services – Consultation Document (8/98)

Code of Practice for Network Operators in Relation to Customer Line Identification Display Services and Other Related Services (2nd edition) – (6/98)

A consumer guide to Calling Line Identification Services – (6/98)

Guidelines on Wiring – Guidelines (2/98)

## NEWSLETTERS, BULLETINS AND OTHER SERIAL PUBLICATIONS

OFTEL News (4 Issues)

Competition Bulletin (4 Issues)

Numbering Bulletin (2 Issues)

Market Information Updates (4 Issues – figures up to March 1998)

# Licences granted in 1998

## PUBLIC TELECOMMUNICATION OPERATORS (PTO's)

| | Date of grant |
|---|---|
| International Computers Limited | June 1998 |
| MLL Telecom Limited | June 1998 |

## NON PTO's

| | |
|---|---|
| Inter Digital Networks Limited (Temporary Licence) | July 1998 |

## INTERNATIONAL FACILITIES

| | |
|---|---|
| Transline Communications Limited | April 1998 |
| Tele Danmark A/S | April 1998 |
| Stentor Communications Limited | April 1998 |
| Startec Global Communications UK Ltd | April 1998 |
| Singtel (Europe) Ltd | April 1998 |
| PSINet Telecom UK Limited | April 1998 |
| o.tel.o communications Limited | April 1998 |
| GN Great Northern Gateway Ltd A/S | April 1998 |
| DirectNet Telecommunications UK Limited | April 1998 |
| Witley Communications Limited | June 1998 |
| Viatel UK Limited | June 1998 |
| Versatel Telecom BV | June 1998 |
| UTG Communications Europe AG | June 1998 |
| Teleport London International Limited | June 1998 |
| Qwest Communications International Limited | June 1998 |
| Internet Network Services Limited | June 1998 |
| International Telecommunications Group Inc. | June 1998 |
| EGN BV | June 1998 |
| Worldport Communications Ltd | August 1998 |
| The JNT Association | August 1998 |
| Telecom One Limited | August 1998 |
| Storm Telecommunications Ltd | August 1998 |
| PT-1 Communications UK Limited | August 1998 |
| NorSea Com AS | August 1998 |
| NETS Limited | August 1998 |
| KPN Telecom UK Limited | August 1998 |
| International Telecom Plc | August 1998 |
| Ibercom Limited | August 1998 |

Continued

| | |
|---|---|
| Eurotunnel Telecommunications Limited | August 1998 |
| Cignal Global Communications UK Ltd | August 1998 |
| Axxon Telecom Limited | September 1998 |
| Zereau Limited | October 1998 |
| NTT Europe Limited | October 1998 |
| Level 3 Communications Limited | October 1998 |
| Data Marine Systems Limited | October 1998 |
| Cyberlight Europe Plc | October 1998 |
| Call-Net (UK) Limited | October 1998 |
| Belgacom UK Limited | October 1998 |
| Alpha Telecom Limited | October 1998 |
| Jersey Telecommunications | December 1998 |
| Japan Telecom UK Limited | December 1998 |
| International Optical Network Limited | December 1998 |
| Flute Limited | December 1998 |
| Eastern Group Telecommunications Limited | December 1998 |
| City Telecom (HK) Limited | December 1998 |

### RADIO PAGING

| | |
|---|---|
| Paging Network (UK) Limited | December 1998 |

### MOBILE DATA

| | |
|---|---|
| Vodafone Value Added & Data Services Ltd | December 1998 |

### INTERNATIONAL SIMPLE VOICE RESALE

| | |
|---|---|
| Alphanet Telecom Inc | February 1998 |
| AXXON Telecom Ltd | February 1998 |
| Darose Ltd | February 1998 |
| Demon Internet Ltd | February 1998 |
| EGN B.V. | February 1998 |
| Force 9 Internet | February 1998 |
| Glocalnet AB | February 1998 |
| Intelligent Network Management Services (UK) Ltd | February 1998 |
| International Telecom Plc | February 1998 |
| LCR Telecom Ltd | February 1998 |
| One Tel Ltd | February 1998 |
| O.Tel.O communications Ltd | February 1998 |

Continued

| | |
|---|---|
| Peach Technologies (Europe) Ltd | February 1998 |
| Phone Systems and Network France | February 1998 |
| Qwest Communications International Ltd | February 1998 |
| Redstone Network Services Ltd | February 1998 |
| Singtel (Europe) Ltd | February 1998 |
| Via-Fon Ltd | February 1998 |
| World-Link Inc | February 1998 |
| Advanced Mobile Communications Ltd | March 1998 |
| Amplefuture Ltd | March 1998 |
| Manorgate (UK) Ltd | March 1998 |
| Phone Home and Away Std Ltd | March 1998 |
| Planetwork International Ltd | March 1998 |
| United Connect Ltd | March 1998 |
| Cable & Wireless Servicos Globais de Cartoes Telefonicos Sociedade Unipessoal Lda (GCS) | April 1998 |
| Centcom Ltd | April 1998 |
| Discount Telecom plc | April 1998 |
| Ecosse Telecommunication Ltd | April 1998 |
| Freephone Telecommunications Ltd | April 1998 |
| Intracom Products (UK) Ltd | April 1998 |
| PT-1 Communications UK Ltd | April 1998 |
| Technology Facility Management plc | April 1998 |
| Tele 2 Europe S.A. | April 1998 |
| The UK Phone Company Ltd | April 1998 |
| Victoria Telecom Ltd | April 1998 |
| Carrier One Ltd | May 1998 |
| Cignal Global Communications UK Ltd | May 1998 |
| Freephone Solutions Ltd | May 1998 |
| KPN Telecom UK Ltd | May 1998 |
| Net Communications Investment Ventures Ltd | May 1998 |
| Ovation Communications plc | May 1998 |
| City Telecom (HK) Ltd | June 1998 |
| Fonorola Ltd | June 1998 |
| Interactive Audiotext Services Ltd | June 1998 |
| Level 3 Communications Ltd | June 1998 |
| Skymaker Ltd | June 1998 |

Continued

| | |
|---|---|
| Swiftcall Ltd | June 1998 |
| Teleconnect Communications International Ltd | June 1998 |
| VarTec Telecom (UK) Ltd | June 1998 |
| Band-X Ltd | July 1998 |
| Belgacom UK Ltd | July 1998 |
| Blue Pacific Telecommunications Ltd | July 1998 |
| Call-Net (UK) Ltd | July 1998 |
| Callmate Telecom Ltd | July 1998 |
| Cellboc Network Protection Ltd | July 1998 |
| Cherry Communications UK Ltd | July 1998 |
| Eurocall Ltd | July 1998 |
| Europa Telecommunications (UK) Ltd | July 1998 |
| Globaltel Ltd | July 1998 |
| Highpoint Telecom Europe plc | July 1998 |
| Instafone plc | July 1998 |
| Nera Ltd | July 1998 |
| Picknet UK plc | July 1998 |
| PLD Telekom Inc | July 1998 |
| Diamond Link Ltd | August 1998 |
| GTS Ltd | August 1998 |
| Microstar Ltd | August 1998 |
| MTU Inform Europe Ltd | August 1998 |
| NextCall Telecom plc (formerly Nextcall UK plc) | August 1998 |
| Nova Vision Ltd | August 1998 |
| Telecom Ltd | August 1998 |
| Telecom UK Phonecard Ltd | August 1998 |
| Telecommunication Ltd | August 1998 |
| Telforce Communications Ltd | August 1998 |
| TNI (Telecom) Ltd | August 1998 |
| Virtual Network Systems (VNS) Ltd | August 1998 |
| Venture Telecommunications Ltd (formerly Level 3 Services) | September 1998 |
| Caldwell Telecommunications Ltd | September 1998 |
| Hadfield Communications Ltd | September 1998 |
| Pathfinder Telecom Ltd | September 1998 |
| Universal Communications (UK) Ltd | September 1998 |
| Allied Communications (UK) Ltd | October 1998 |

Continued

| | |
|---|---|
| Call UK Ltd | October 1998 |
| CMM Telecommunications company Ltd | October 1998 |
| CompleTel UK Ltd | October 1998 |
| Comtech International UK Ltd | October 1998 |
| Intelnet Communications Ltd | October 1998 |
| Pantheon Telecom (UK) Ltd | October 1998 |
| Ringmaster Ltd | October 1998 |
| Speed 7189 Ltd | October 1998 |
| Stanhope Telecommunications Ltd | October 1998 |
| Syntec UK Ltd | October 1998 |
| Unitel Communications | October 1998 |
| USA Global Link (UK) Ltd | October 1998 |
| World Telecom Plc | October 1998 |
| ACN European Services Ltd | November 1998 |
| Global First Ltd | November 1998 |
| ICS France SA | November 1998 |
| Whizz Telecommunications Ltd | November 1998 |
| Xplorium Ltd | November 1998 |
| Ambro International Ltd | December 1998 |
| Apple Telecom International Ltd | December 1998 |
| GC Global Communications Ltd | December 1998 |
| Iomart Ltd | December 1998 |
| Macfarlane Telesystems Ltd | December 1998 |
| Madge Networks Ltd | December 1998 |
| Mastercall Telecommunications Ltd | December 1998 |
| Netkonect Communications Ltd | December 1998 |
| The Postmodem Company Ltd | December 1998 |
| ZHL Ltd | December 1998 |

# Background Statistics

## 1. EXCHANGE CONNECTIONS AND CALLS

**1.1** Exchange connections in service by type of subscriber
(1984 -1998 United Kingdom) – directly connected lines only

| Year (at 31 March) | Total (000s) | Residential customers (000s) | Business customers (000s) |
|---|---|---|---|
| 1984* | 19,812 | 16,044 | 3,768 |
| 1985* | 20,528 | 16,596 | 3,932 |
| 1986* | 21,261 | 17,120 | 4,141 |
| 1987* | 21,908 | 17,549 | 4,359 |
| 1988* | 22,664 | 18,106 | 4,558 |
| 1989* | 23,740 | 18,703 | 5,037 |
| 1990* | 24,797 | 19,246 | 5,551 |
| 1991* | 25,368 | 19,573 | 5,795 |
| 1992 | 25,911 | 19,882 | 6,029 |
| 1993 | 26,514 | 20,346 | 6,168 |
| 1994 | 27,336 | 20,943 | 6,393 |
| 1995 | 28,358 | 21,538 | 6,820 |
| 1996 | 29,410 | 22,111 | 7,299 |
| 1997 | 30,678 | 22,777 | 7,091 |
| 1998 | 31,878 | 23,412 | 8,466 |

*Figures for these years relate to BT only. 1992 onward figures relate to all operators in the UK

**Source:** Oftel Market Information, February 1999

**1.2** Payphones in service by type (1984, 1986-1998 UK)

| Year (at 31 March) | BT public payphones[1] (000s) | Other operator public payphones[1,2] (000s) | All operators private rented payphones (000s) |
|---|---|---|---|
| 1984 | 77 | n.a. | 286* |
| 1985 | | | |
| 1986 | 77 | n.a. | 296* |
| 1987 | 78 | n.a. | 306* |
| 1988 | 81 | n.a. | 320* |
| 1989 | 86 | n.a. | 358* |
| 1990 | 90 | n.a. | 286* |
| 1991 | 96 | n.a. | 260* |
| 1992 | 105.5 | 1.2 | 242.7 |
| 1993 | 113.0 | 1.3 | 216.3 |
| 1994 | 123.7 | 1.5 | 187.2 |
| 1995 | 129.1 | 1.9 | 162.3 |
| 1996 | 133.7 | 6.4 | 146.5 |
| 1997 | 136.7 | 8.9 | 197.6** |
| 1998 | 138.8 | 8.7 | 193.7** |

n.a. not available

[1] Figures include the operator's 'managed' payphones, ie those installed at stations or airports and managed by BT or other operators. Public and managed payphones are those payphones where the public telecommunications operator sets the tariff and collects all the revenues generated by the payphone.

[2] Figures relate to Mercury, Kingston Communications, New World Payphones and IPM Communications, 31 March 1992 was the earliest date for which data were collected.

* Figures relate to BT only.

** Private payphone figures for 1997 are based on the number of private payphone exchange lines. Previous figures relate to the number of actual private payphones.

**Source:** Oftel Market Information, February 1999.

**1.3** Revenues from fixed link telephony (excluding payphones) by service – all operators (shown in £million)

| | Year to 31 March: | | | | |
| | 1994 | 1995 | 1996 | 1997 | 1998 |
|---|---|---|---|---|---|
| **(a) Simple voice message conveyance** | | | | | |
| Local calls | 2,235 | 2,168 | 2,150 | 2,209 | 2,211 |
| National calls | 2,373 | 2,144 | 2,061 | 1,955 | 1,837 |
| International calls | 1,291 | 1,350 | 1,418 | 1,478 | 1,452 |
| Calls to mobiles | 343 | 446 | 593 | 673 | 972 |
| Other calls* | 1,061 | 1,082 | 1,122 | 1,207 | 1,473 |
| All calls | 7,304 | 7,190 | 7,343 | 7,521 | 7945 |
| **(b) Exchange line connections** | | | | | |
| Business customers | 100 | 129 | 141 | 150 | 155 |
| Residential customers | 107 | 101 | 89 | 93 | 89 |
| Total | 207 | 230 | 229 | 243 | 243 |
| **(c) Exchange line rentals** | | | | | |
| Business customers | 785 | 965 | 1,066 | 1,105 | 1,224 |
| Residential customers | 1,565 | 1,657 | 1,767 | 1,833 | 1,934 |
| Total | 2,350 | 2,622 | 2,832 | 2,938 | 3,157 |
| **TOTAL REVENUES** | **9,150** | **9,635** | **10,010** | **10,702** | **11,345** |

*This category includes calls to freefone services, special local rate services, premium rate services, national and international directory enquiries and 'other' calls through the operator.

**Source:** Oftel Market Information, February 1999.

**1.4** Retail call minutes on fixed link telephony, by type of call – all operators (shown in millions of minutes)

| | Year to 31 March: | | | | |
| | 1994 | 1995 | 1996 | 1997 | 1998 |
|---|---|---|---|---|---|
| **Simple voice message conveyance** | | | | | |
| Local calls | 68,020 | 72,825 | 79,367 | 86,280 | 90,070 |
| National calls | 31,239 | 34,258 | 37,265 | 39,730 | 43,576 |
| Outgoing international calls | 3,230 | 3,623 | 4,068 | 4,539 | 5,490 |
| Calls to mobiles | 1,124 | 1,608 | 2,388 | 2,819 | 3,787 |
| Other calls* | 1,804 | 2,246 | 2,814 | 5,019 | 11,887 |
| All calls | 105,416 | 114,560 | 125,901 | 138,386 | 154,809 |

*This category includes calls to freefone services, special local rate services, premium rate services, national and international directory enquiries and 'other' calls through the operator.

**Source:** Oftel Market Information, February 1999.

**1.5** Leased lines – revenues and numbers:

| Revenues (£m) | 1994 | 1995 | Year to 31 March: 1996 | 1997 | 1998 |
|---|---|---|---|---|---|
| **(a) Inland – leased line connections** | | | | | |
| Analogue | 52 | 50 | 41 | 31 | 21 |
| Digital* | 42 | 64 | 77 | 89 | 104 |
| Total | 94 | 114 | 118 | 120 | 125 |
| **(b) Inland – leased line rentals** | | | | | |
| Analogue | 435 | 396 | 335 | 311 | 253 |
| Digital* | 448 | 519 | 619 | 724 | 833 |
| Total | 883 | 915 | 954 | 1,035 | 1,086 |
| **(c) International – leased line rentals** | | | | | |
| Analogue | 31 | 29 | 24 | 16 | 12 |
| Digital* | 136 | 148 | 210 | 285 | 310 |
| Total | 167 | 177 | 234 | 301 | 322 |
| **(d) Inland – number at end of year (000s)** | | | | | |
| Analogue | n.a. | 420 | 382 | 364 | 263 |
| Digital* | n.a. | 121 | 137 | 156 | 187 |
| **(e) International – number at end of year (000s)** | | | | | |
| Analogue | 3.6 | 3.1 | 2.6 | 1.5 | 1.3 |
| Digital* | n.a. | 5.4 | 5.9 | 5.7 | 7.1 |

*All capacities

**Source:** Oftel Market Information, February 1999.

**1.6** Cellular telephony

| | 1994 | 1995 | Year to 31 March: 1996 | 1997 | 1998 |
|---|---|---|---|---|---|
| **Revenues from customers (£m)*** | | | | | |
| Connections | 32 | 59 | 48 | 74 | 74 |
| Rentals and calls | 1,162 | 1,579 | 2,218 | 2,674 | 3,129 |
| Total | 1,194 | 1,639 | 2,266 | 2,748 | 3,203 |
| **Call minutes (£ms)** | 2,047 | 3,359 | 5,059 | 6,806 | 9,572 |
| **Number of subscribers at end of year (000s)** | 2,266 | 3,940 | 5,736 | 7,109 | 9,023 |

*These figures represent the revenues paid direct by customers and not those paid by service providers to network operators as shown in previous Annual Reports.

**Source:** Oftel Market Information, February 1999.

## 2. BT's Quality of Service
### 2.1 Network reliability (1994-1998)

| | % UK call failures due to BT |
|---|---|
| April 1994 – June 1994 | 0.12 |
| July 1994 – Sept 1994 | 0.14 |
| Oct 1994 – Dec 1994 | 0.15 |
| Jan 1995 – June 1995 | 0.21 |
| April 1995 – June 1995 | 0.16 |
| July 1995 – Sept 1995 | 0.23 |
| Oct 1995 – Dec 1995 | 0.24 |
| Jan 1996 – March 1996 | 0.33 |
| April 1996 – June 1996 | 0.30 |
| July 1996 – Sept 1996 | 0.27 |
| April 1997 – June 1997 | 0.30 |
| July 1997 – Sept 1997 | 0.31 |
| Oct 1997 – Dec 1997 | 0.38 |
| Jan 1998 – March 1998 | 0.56 |
| April 1998 – June 1998 | 0.48 |
| July 1998 – Sept 1998 | 0.42 |

**Source:** BT

### 2.2 Fault repair service (1990-1998)

| | Percentage of faults cleared within 2 working days | |
|---|---|---|
| | **Business** | **Residential** |
| April 1991 – Sept 1991 | 99.3 | 98.3 |
| Oct 1991 – March 1992 | 99.4 | 98.6 |
| April 1992 – Sept 1992 | 98.7 | 98.0 |
| Oct 1992 – March 1993 | 98.3 | 95.3 |
| April 1993 – Sept 1993 | 98.9 | 96.8 |
| Oct 1993 – March 1994 | 98.8 | 94.0 |
| April 1994 – Sept 1994 | 98.9 | 95.1 |
| Oct 1994 – March 1995 | 98.9 | 92.0 |
| April 1995 – Sept 1995 | 99.1 | 95.9 |
| Oct 1995 – March 1996 | 99.2 | 96.3 |
| April 1996 – Sept 1996 | 99.1 | 96.7 |
| Oct 1996 – March 1997 | 98.7 | 93.3 |
| April 1997 – Sept 1997 | 98.8 | 94.0 |
| Oct 1997 – March 1998 | 98.6 | 92.6 |
| April 1998 – Sept 1998 | 98.9 | 95.0 |

**Source:** BT

**2.3** Operator services and directory enquiries (1990-1998)

| | Operator calls answered in 15 secs (%) | Directory enquiries answered in 15 secs (%) |
|---|---|---|
| 1984 | 86.0 | n.a. |
| Oct 1990 – March 1991 | 88.8 | 89.4 |
| April 1991 – Sept 1991 | 90.1 | 94.1 |
| Oct 1991 – March 1992 | 94.0 | 92.8 |
| April 1992 – Sept 1992 | 91.4 | 83.7 |
| Oct 1992 – March 1993 | 93.0 | 92.5 |
| April 1993 – Sept 1993 | 91.0 | 89.3 |
| Oct 1993 – March 1994 | 90.7 | 90.1 |
| April 1994 – Sept 1994 | 90.4 | 90.3 |
| Oct 1994 – March 1995 | 91.4 | 92.0 |
| April 1995 – Sept 1995 | 88.0 | 90.6 |
| Oct 1995 – March 1996 | 91.9 | 92.0 |
| April 1996 – Sept 1996 | 88.0 | 87.8 |
| Oct 1996 – March 1997 | 92.1 | 91.1 |
| April 1997 – Sept 1997 | 85.1 | 91.3 |
| Oct 1997 – March 1998 | 89.9 | 91.4 |
| April 1998 – Sept 1998 | 91.8 | 91.0 |
| **Source:** BT | | |

## 3. TELEGRAPH AND TELECOMMUNICATIONS EQUIPMENT INDUSTRY DATA

**3.1** Estimated numbers of facsimile terminals (1986-1996 UK)

| | Number (000s) |
|---|---|
| December 1986 | 86 |
| December 1987 | 173 |
| December 1988 | 370 |
| December 1989 | 556 |
| December 1990 | 750 |
| December 1991 | 920 |
| December 1992 | 1,065 |
| December 1993 | 1,195 |
| December 1994 | 1,425 |
| December 1995 | 1,747 |
| December 1996 | 1,992 |

These figures are no longer being collected, therefore there is no new data for 1997 or 1998.

**Source:** British Facsimile Industry Consultative Committee (BFICC)

**3.2** Proportion of new PABXs and key systems supplied by BT (based on number of extension lines supplied) by size of system (1980-1997)

| Year to 31st March | Small systems (%) | Medium systems (%) | Large systems (%) | Total systems (%) |
|---|---|---|---|---|
| 1980-1981 | 99 | 87 | 0 | 83 |
| 1981-1982 | 100 | 92 | 0 | 81 |
| 1982-1983 | 97 | 85 | 1 | 74 |
| 1983-1984 | 95 | 80 | 17 | 76 |
| 1984-1985 | 95 | 75 | 48 | 75 |
| 1985-1986 | 84 | 63 | 52 | 69 |
| 1986-1987 | 78 | 50 | 37 | 58 |
| 1987* | 68 | 43 | 38 | 52 |
| 1988* | 65 | 45 | 37 | 51 |
| 1989* | 59 | 43 | 37 | 47 |
| 1990* | 50 | 35 | 38 | 40 |
| 1991* | 45 | 35 | 33 | 38 |
| 1992* | 49 | 27 | 24 | 35 |
| 1993* | 48 | 23 | 22 | 30 |
| 1994* | 41 | 36 | 25 | 29 |
| 1995* | 41 | 27 | 25 | 29 |
| 1996* | 22 | 25 | 56 | 27 |
| 1997* | 26 | 26 | 30 | 26 |

Notes: Small systems – up to 16 lines; Medium systems – 17 to 500 lines; Large systems over 500 lines
*Figures for the years from 1987 onwards relate to January to December.

**Sources:** 1981-1985: The Monopolies and Mergers Commission, British Telecommunications plc and Mitel Corporation, a report on the proposed merger, HMSO 1986 (Cmnd 9715) 1986 – 1997; MZA Consultants.

**3.3** Proportion of new telephones and telephone answering machines supplied by BT
(ex manufacturers' deliveries) (1984-1997)

| Year to 31 March | Telephones (%) | Telephone answering # machines (%) |
| --- | --- | --- |
| 1984-1985 | 83 | n.a |
| 1985-1986 | 79 | 25 |
| 1986-1987 | 66 | 25 |
| 1987* | 54 | 30 |
| 1988* | 51 | 40 |
| 1989* | 50 | 43 |
| 1990* | 54 | 29 |
| 1991* | 53 | 46 |
| 1992* | 48 | 46 |
| 1993* | 55 | 62 |
| 1994* | 54 | 57 |
| 1995* | 52 | 56 |
| 1996* | 48 | 57 |
| 1997* | 50 | 49 |

*Figures for the years 1987 onwards relate to January to December

#Including Teltams

n.a. Not available

**Source:** MZA Consultants

# List of orders, directions and determinations during 1998

| CASE DETAIL | DATE OF ISSUE & ENFORCEMENT INSTRUMENT | LICENCE BREACH IDENTIFIED |
|---|---|---|
| (1) **Apparatus Supply Business direction** | 6.12.91 Direction | Breach of C18. BT's Apparatus Supply Business constituted a monopoly situation under the Fair Trading Act 1973. The ASB was receiving unfair cross-subsidy because it had failed to make an adequate return after covering its fully allocated costs. This constituted a breach of C18 of BT's licence which prohibits BT from unfairly cross-subsidising its ASB. |
| (2) **BT's Sunday Special Offer** | 2.8.93 Determination | Breach of C.17. BT's Sunday Special tariff failed to cover the costs of network usage if those were assessed on basis used for other operators interconnecting with the BT network. Competing operators incurred higher network costs than BT. BT acted unduly discriminatorily in unfairly favouring its own business to a material extent and placing interconnecting operators at a significant disadvantage. |
| (3) **Telephone Equipment Direction : BT** | 22.9.95 Direction | Breach of C.20B.15. Unfair subsidy of BT's network Business as a whole and certain parts of that Business. BT's share of the market for the supply of the products in question (eg corded/cordless telephones , telephone answering machines etc) was such that its behaviour was likely to inhibit competition and damage its competitors by limiting the prices they could charge to uneconomic levels. |
| (4) **Satellite uplinking:BT** | 1.11.95 Final Order | Breach of C.16 – BT failed to publish a notice regarding its backhaul circuits. Breach of C.17 – BT failed to make available/offer its competitors the backhaul circuit service it provides/offers to its own satellite up-linking business. |
| (5) **Clifford Chance complaint against BTMNS** | 7.2.96 Direction | Breach of C.20B.15. Inadequate accounting controls within BT's core business over charges to other parts of BT (eg MNS). Unfair subsidy/cross subsidy of parts of the MNS Business. |
| (6) **CLI Special Offers : BT** | 26.6.96 Provisional Order (confirmed 25.9.96-see entry no 8) | Breach of C.17. BT failed to give Caller Display Equipment suppliers sufficient advance notice of an intended offer to customers regarding its Caller Display Service. Preference/discrimination occurred where BT discussed the promotion with one existing and one prospective supplier before general notification of offer to other suppliers. Discussions between BT's Systems Business and BT's Apparatus Supply Business before general notification of the promotion to other equipment suppliers materially favoured BT's own Caller Display Equipment business. |

LIST OF ORDERS, DIRECTIONS, DETERMINATIONS

| | | |
|---|---|---|
| (7) Denigration of competitors: BT | 3.9.96 Provisional Order (not confirmed) | Breach of C.17. BT gave misleading/inaccurate information concerning the costs of its services/available discounts and concerning comparisons with the call charges of competing cable operators. |
| (8) CLI Special Offers: BT | 25.9.96 (confirmed Final Order) | For details see entry no 6 above re CLI Special Offers. |
| (9) BT/BSkyB Marketing Agreement | 22.10.96 Provisional Order (not confirmed) | Breach of C.17. BT made an unduly preferential offer towards its own customers and those of BSkyB. By picking up BSkyB's advertising costs BT was effectively funding free calls for those taking up the offer in whole or in part. |
| (10) Ring Back When Free: BT | 3.12.96 Determination | Breach of C.17. In trialing its 'Ring Back When Free' service BT favoured its own Pay Phone Business over competitors' businesses by failing to give adequate notice of the service to known manufacturers and suppliers of pay phone equipment in sufficient time to enable them to adapt their equipment etc to take account of it. |
| (11) Discount on calls Marketing/advertising campaign | (Re-connection Offer) 3.3.97 Provisional Order (confirmed 24.6.97-see entry no 13) | Breach of C.17. BT ran a marketing campaign offering discounts on calls, aiming it in a discriminatory manner at those who had left BT for other operators. In failing to obtain the necessary permission from the Director General for below cost pricing BT also breached C24F.4. |
| (12) Installation of payphone lines for Maintel's private call box sites: BT | 15.4.97 Determination | Breach of C.17. BT failed to supply and install lines timeously and efficiently to competing operators of private call boxes. Such inefficiency in supplying payphone lines to itself has little or no impact on the revenues/profitability of BT's payphone business, but can have material impact on the success or viability of smaller operators who are dependent on BT for the necessary connection/access services. |
| (13) Discount on calls Marketing/advertising campaign | (Re-connection Offer) 24.6.97 Final Order | For details see entry no 11 above re discounts on calls marketing/advertising campaign. In confirming the provisional order made on 3.3.97, the Director was satisfied that BT is likely again to contravene these conditions unless an order is made to enforce them. |

| | | |
|---|---|---|
| **(14) BT's Chargecard prices** | 3.7.97<br>Initial Determination<br>(C18A) and<br>Provisional Order.<br>(not confirmed) | BT breached C18A. BT has a dominant position in the post paid calling card market. Setting retail prices at such a low level for both local and national calls, as to be below its operational costs for providing Chargecard service ( which includes PPSCC -payphone access levy) constitutes unfair pricing and is an abuse in the Chargecard market. |
| **(15) BT's Call Minder** | 23.9.97<br>Provisional Order.<br>(confirmed<br>19.12.97-see entry<br>no 18) | BT breached C17. BT in providing Call Minder from the SB as a bundled service, and in not operating the voice messaging element of the service from the SSB, and in not making available the relevant network inputs to third parties wishing to compete with Call Minder, it is unfairly favouring a business carried by it to a material extent. This constitutes a breach of C17 of BT's licence. |
| **(16) BT's OneNumber** | 23.9.97<br>Provisional Order.<br>(not confirmed) | BT breached C17. BT in providing the voicemail element of OneNumber from the SB and not from the SSB, and in not making available the relevant network inputs to third parties wishing to compete with OneNumber's voicemail, it is unfairly favouring a business carried by it to a material extent. This constitutes a breach of C17 of BT's licence. |
| **(17) BT's Broadcast Sound Services** | 29.9.97<br>Provisional Order.<br>(not confirmed) | BT breached Cs 1,17&23. BT by structuring the MusicLine 2000 tariff according to capacity available, rather than according to actual use made by the customer of that capacity is in contravention of C17.1; BT's proposed price increase for EPS products, which it proposes to withdraw in June 1998 and not offering customers a reasonably priced alternative constitutes contravention of C1; BT by not publishing a Suppliers Information Note for its MusicLine service is in breach of C23. |
| **(18) BT's Call Minder** | 19.12.97<br>Confirmed Final<br>Order | For details see entry no 15 above re BT's Call Minder. In confirming the provisional order made on 23.9.97, the Director was satisfied that BT was likely again to contravene this condition because, among other things, it had not yet been able to show to him that its internal compliance procedures would effectively ensure that there would not be any further contravention of C17 in relation to the services covered by the order. |
| **(19) BT's Price List** | 12.2.98<br>Final Order | BT breached C16.1(a)(i). BT by the omission of the charges for certain FeatureNet Ancillary Services, Broadcast Services – Vision Circuits National- BTCNAPs and RedCARE Alarms from its Price List had failed in complying with its obligation under C16.1(a)(i) of its licnece and therefore is in contravention of that condition. |

LIST OF ORDERS, DIRECTIONS, DETERMINATIONS

| (20) Cellnet's Service Provider Payment Plan | 12.2.98 Provisional Order (not confirmed) | Cellnet breached Cs 1, 9 and 37. Cellnet by offering a new Service Provider Payment Plan whose bonus and discount structure served to show undue preference towards tied service providers with ownership ties to Cellnet at the expense of smaller independent service providers. This constitutes a breach of Cs 1, 9 and 37 of its licence. |
|---|---|---|
| (21) The British Fax Directory's faxfinding activities | 27.5.1998 Final Order | Launchasset Ltd trading as The British Fax Directory (BFD) breached C6.2(a) of the Telecommunications Services Licence(TSL). BFD used automatic calling equipment to initiate calls for the purpose of identifying whether apparatus addressed by the number so called is capable of the transmission or reception of facsimile messages without obtaining prior consent in writing from the recipient of the call. This constitutes a breach of C6.2(a) of the TSL. |

**NOTE:** For copies of orders, directions and determinations see BP/050/001

Frontline Design • Covent Garden • London • WC2E 8JS
Printed in the UK for The Stationery Office Limited on behalf of the
Controller of Her Majesty's Stationery Office
Dd 5068798   4/99   19585   Job No 79892   424851